# The Cheesemonger's Tales

# The Cheesemonger's Tales

ARTHUR CUNYNGHAME

An eclectic mix of delightful anecdotes
and helpful information, based around
a personal selection of twelve of the finest cheeses,
and the people who make them,
matched with twelve memorable wines;
and much more.

First published in Great Britain in 2006
Reprinted 2007

Loose Chippings Books
The Paddocks
Chipping Campden
Gloucestershire
GL55 6AU

Printed and bound by J.H.Haynes, Sparkford, England

ISBN 978-0-9554217-0-9

# SNAPSHOTS OF MY LIFE IN FOOD & WINE

It wasn't so much that I wanted to be a wine merchant as that I couldn't be a film producer. Having left school with three 'A' levels and the usual batch of 'O' levels and deciding I didn't want to go to university, I sat down, like a great many 17 year olds, to try and decide what I did want to do. Film producing was one thing I definitely did fancy, due partly, I suppose, to my father's involvement with Alexander Korda, the great Hungarian producer, and my mother's acting career playing a number of roles, chief of which, as far as I could see, was Queen Victoria.

It soon became apparent that I was not going to be the new David Lean as I so fervently hoped. It seems to me now, that other people recognised something I failed to see myself; that, much though I longed to be in films, I didn't have the absolute and total commitment which is necessary to sustain one through the inevitable disappointments which are such an integral part of the entertainment business before, if one is lucky, the 'right' vehicle arrives to boost ones fortunes and self confidence.

It was therefore through a lack of anything better to do that I agreed to 'help out' my brother, John, at MacDonald Hall & Co Ltd over Christmas 1968 and into 1969. At that time the company was really a vehicle for any business which might profitably be undertaken; selling steel to Greece, dealing with the Saudis, marketing pneumatic tools, and of course wine! Over the years that followed I was lucky enough to pursue a life in wine and then cheese.

John and I bought the wine business. I was determined not to have a desk job and was happy enough for a time assembling and delivering orders and doing a bit of everything. It was good fun and what a way to learn about business.

The life to which I aspired was that of most of our suppliers. They arrived in their offices at about 10, did a little work, went out to lunch at 12 and that was more or less their day. They might have returned to their office for a post prandial snooze between 4 and 5 but the only time I could get hold of anyone in authority was for 2 hours each morning.

Of the many tastings, which I attended, there is no doubt that one of the most special was the annual tasting given by H. Sichel & Son, actually in their cellars underneath London Bridge railway station. The cellars were transformed from working cellars, by the installation of candelabra, and tables spread with white linen cloths and fine silver. The wines didn't usually disappoint either.

After 4 years of running the wine business with my brother, we decided that it was time one or other of us knew something about wine! I volunteered to go off and work in the vineyards of France for 6 months.

In 1977, we bought a business in Leamington Spa. It was a wine company run in the former malthouse of the old Thornley Kelsey brewery. The parent company was about to close the business and make everyone redundant. They seemed quite surprised and pleased that anyone should want to buy it! However, the buying involved them paying us to take it off their hands. I moved to Leamington to run it.

# SNAPSHOTS OF MY LIFE IN FOOD & WINE

We sold the wine business to the hotel giant, Trusthouse Forte. It was the first time I had worked for a large company; too much politics, too little assumption of responsibility, too much bureaucracy, too little encouragement of initiative.

I bought a cheese business at the end of the 1980's. Rachel & I ran it from our house, with storage in two refrigerated containers at my mother-in-law's farm just over the hill. From that we progressed to a shop in Stratford-upon-Avon.

Rachel and I enrolled in night classes to learn the basics of cheesemaking. We went to a fabulous old Victorian dairy (part of Worcester Agricultural College). There were beautiful ceramic tiles on the walls, and a high ceiling with louvered vents to allow the room to stay cool. I discovered that cheesemaking is an enticing mix of art and science. The best cheeses are works of art, but the making is based on science.

I had the opportunity to buy the venerable old firm of Paxton & Whitfield, which was going through something of a lean patch. We built the business and Paxton & Whitfield became, once more, respected for its quality.

Judging at cheese competitions in Britain and France was part of my life as a cheesemonger as well as conducting many cheese and wine master-classes, including two in Tokyo.

Many people put in a lot of effort at Paxton's and it was a singular honour to be granted Royal Warrants first to The Prince of Wales and then to The Queen. Then the time came to sell and I accepted an offer for the business.

# CONTENTS

*The chapters follow the order of cheeses I like to use for tutored tastings, ranging from the milder flavours towards the stronger. Each cheese is matched with a wine, and I have included general information throughout the book.*

# SETTING THE SCENE

### ❖ Matching Cheese & Wine

Cheese and wine are perfect partners and the right combination can add to the enjoyment of both. During the time I owned Paxton & Whitfield Ltd, the cheesemongers, I conducted many tutored cheese & wine tastings, including two in Tokyo which proved enormously popular. In this book I have attempted to capture the essence of what proved so popular on so many evenings.

Balance is essential in pairing cheese and wine. Neither should overpower the other; their strength of flavour should be roughly equal. If a cheese has a particularly complex set of flavours, as most great cheeses do, often the wine which matches it best will be a relatively simple straightforward one; two sets of complex flavours are sometimes too much to cope with. One of the first things I came to realise is that, although some red wines are magical partners to certain cheeses and ports can be especially good, white wines are often the best match for particular cheeses. Now, that is all very well in a tutored tasting but the problem comes in eating cheese after a main course when red wine has been served. Moving to a lighter wine from a heavier wine does not provide a pleasant sequence, so we tend to serve red wines. I find the answer then is to choose a cheese or cheeses which will complement the red wine. If the main course has been light and accompanied by a white wine, then it is very satisfactory to continue with white wine for the cheese, provided the right style of cheese is chosen.

When seeking to match wines with cheeses, it is as well to be prepared for many surprises. There are few hard and fast rules and just when you think you know a wine which will partner a cheese perfectly, it turns out to be a disaster; and when you think a combination is likely to be poor, you are often pleasantly surprised. Nonetheless, over the years, I have developed several rules of thumb. Wines which work well with cheese tend to have: good fruit (often with a touch of sweetness, though not too raisiny), good acidity (which is essential to cut through the fat of the cheese), and low tannin. Wines which are difficult with cheese are those with high tannins or too much oak.

Grape varieties are often a better guide to good or bad combinations than geographical origin but, having said that, cheeses and wines produced in the same region are often, literally, made for each other.

I have found that the grape varieties which tend to go well with cheese include: Pinot Noir, Cabernet Franc, Semillon, Viognier, Riesling, Muscat and Gewurztraminer. Difficult grape varieties include, perhaps surprisingly, Cabernet Sauvignon and Chardonnay.

## ❖ Cheese & Wine Parallels

As well as being perfect partners on the table, cheese and wine closely mirror each other in their production. Climate and soil have an effect on both. The breed of animal can be said to equate to the grape variety and the stage of lactation of the animal has parallels with the age of the vine. What the animal is fed loosely corresponds to the pruning of the vine. And so we have our 'raw material', milk and grapes. Whilst milk differs every day, winemakers can consider themselves fortunate that they have only one vintage a year. Although the actual cheesemaking process is different from winemaking, there are, nonetheless, parallels. Finally, we come to the ageing or maturation which, of course, applies to both cheese and wine.

### ❖ Cheese & Wine Master-classes

One of the first Master-classes in Cheese & Wine Matching, which I conducted, was with George Sandeman of Sandeman's Port. The cheese and port pairings were superb and set the theme for many successful future tastings.

In 1997 Peter McKinley and I did a fascinating tasting of cheeses with various spirits. Some of the flavour matches were superb but I was left with the feeling that more liquid was needed to wash down the cheese than was provided by the spirits – unless one was going to get very emotional indeed.

Over the years The Wine Society produced some splendid wines to accompany my cheeses and we held the tastings in some glorious venues – including the Assembly Rooms in Bath, a particularly splendid setting.

One of the most interesting tastings I conducted was with Remi Krug; certainly a tasting to blow away misconceptions. Krug Champagne went magnificently with cheeses which I least expected, and was less successful with those I thought would work well.

Tastings with Berry Bros always seemed as near perfection as one could wish. For a start, the approach of the two firms was very compatible; secondly, Lance Jefferson and I seemed to strike up a very congenial and effective way of working together; and most importantly, the quality of the Berry wines shone through to complement my cheeses. These were happy events and they were always sold out. Most were conducted in Berry's splendidly refurbished cellars under 3 St James's Street. It was always a pleasure to walk through their doors and breathe in the sense of timelessness which permeates the place. However, we also took our show to Japan, where two tastings at The British Embassy and The Tokyo America Club were outstanding successes.

## ❖ Wines to go with cheeses

*Hard Mild Cheeses* such as Wensleydale and Cheshire go well with many white wines such as a Sancerre, Pinot Blanc and Chardonnay and light, fruity reds such as a Beaujolais or other Gamay wines.

*Hard Mature Cheeses* such as Cheddar and Gruyère go well with fuller whites such as Viognier or Gewurztraminer, sweet whites such as a Quart de Chaume or medium reds such as a bold Cabernet Franc, Merlot or Cabernet Sauvignon.

*Soft Cheeses* such as Brie de Meaux and Camembert are especially good with Red Burgundies or other Pinot Noir wines, Cabernet Franc wines from the Loire like Chinon and the lighter fortified wines such as a 10 year old Tawny Port.

*Full-Flavoured Pungent Cheeses* like Epoisses or Pont L'Evêque are usually well suited to sweet whites such as Pinot Gris Vendange Tardive or Sauternes, full-bodied reds like Châteauneuf-du-pape and fortified wines such as Vintage Port.

*Blue Cheeses* such as Stilton, Fourme d'Ambert, Gorgonzola and Roquefort find natural partners in most sweet whites especially Sauternes, full bodied reds such as Barolo, and fortified wines especially Vintage Port.

*Goats' Milk Cheeses* such as Valençay, Crottin de Chavignol and Golden Cross are ideally matched to crisp dry whites such as Sauvignon, occasionally to fuller whites like Pinot Blanc and light reds such as Chinon.

*Sheep's Milk Cheeses* such as Wigmore and Berkswell are perfect with a 20-Year-Old Tawny Port, fuller whites, sweet whites such as Côteaux de Layon and some medium reds such as a Tempranillo.

## ❖ Cheeses to go with wines

*Crisp Dry White Wines* such as Sauvignon, Chenin Blanc Sec and Riesling are ideal with goats' cheeses like Golden Cross and Valençay as well as mild hard cheeses like Wensleydale.

*Full White Wines* such as Chardonnay, Gewurztraminer and Viognier go well with hard cheeses like Double Gloucester and Parmigiano Reggiano, some full-flavoured pungent cheeses, and many hard sheep's and goats' cheeses.

*Champagne,* if it is full-bodied, can be enjoyed with many hard cheeses especially mountain cheeses like Beaufort and Comté, as well as some of the full-flavoured pungent cheeses such as Maroilles.

*Sweet White Wines* such as Semillon and Chenin Blanc Demi Sec are natural partners to most blue cheeses especially Roquefort, some mature hard cows' and sheep's cheeses and full-flavoured pungent cheeses such as Munster.

*Light Red Wines* like Pinot Noir, Gamay and Cabernet Franc go well with soft cheeses such as Brie de Meaux and St Marcellin, hard mild cheeses such as Cheshire or Red Leicester, and a few goats' cheeses.

*Medium Red Wines* like Merlot and Cabernet Sauvignon go well with British hard cheeses such as Cheddar and Single Gloucester.

*Full-bodied Red Wines* like Syrah and Grenache go well with full-flavoured pungent cheeses such as Pont L'Evêque and many blue cheeses like Fourme d'Ambert and Gorgonzola.

*Light Fortified Wines* like White Port and Old Tawny port are good matches for mild hard cheeses from all milks and many soft or crumbly cheeses.

*Full Fortified Wines* such as Vintage Port are, perhaps, the most versatile, going well with cheeses such as Stilton, other blues, full-flavoured pungent cheeses, some soft cheeses, certain goats' cheeses and hard nibbling cheeses.

## ❖ Flavour & Aroma

Describing flavours is one of the hardest things to do. Firstly, you have to have a good memory for what you have tasted before and secondly, you need some lateral thinking to link the flavour of a cheese with the flavour of, say, a fruit or a vegetable. Here are some descriptive words, which you may find useful.

## LACTIC

| | |
|---|---|
| Fresh Lactic | Fresh Milk, Curd, Cream, Butter |
| Acidified Lactic | Yoghurt, Whey, Sour |
| Heated Lactic | Melted Butter, Boiled Milk, Rancid |

## VEGETABLE

| | |
|---|---|
| Grass | New mown grass, Hay, Silage |
| Herbs | Tarragon, Basil, Thyme, Coriander, Mint |
| Spices | Clove, Nutmeg, Pepper, Chilli |
| Fungal | Mushrooms, Truffle, Mouldy |
| Boiled Vegetables | Cabbage, Celery, Peas |
| Root Vegetables | Potato, Parsnip, Beetroot, Carrot |
| Bulb Vegetables | Onion, Garlic |

## FLORAL

| | |
|---|---|
| Flowers | Rose, Violet |

## NUTS

| | |
|---|---|
| Fresh | Hazelnut, Walnut, Chestnut, Almond |
| Roasted | Almond, Peanut, Hazelnut |

## FRUIT

| | |
|---|---|
| Citrus Fruits | Orange, Lemon, Grapefruit |
| Tropical Fruits | Banana, Pineapple, Melon, Mango |
| Stone or Pip Fruits | Apricot, Apple, Pear, Peach, Plum |
| Berries | Blackcurrant, Strawberry, Gooseberry |
| Processed Fruits | Dried Fruits, Fermented Fruits |

## TOASTED

| | |
|---|---|
| Light Toasted | Vanilla, Brioche |
| Medium Toasted | Toffee, Chicory, Coffee, Chocolate |
| Strong Toast | Smokey, Burnt |

## ANIMAL

| | |
|---|---|
| Bovine | Cow Shed, Leather, Sweat |
| Meat | Meat Broth, Beefy, Gamey |
| Manure | Bovine Manure |

## OTHER

Sulphur, Ammonia, Mouldy, Musty, Salt, Malt, Marmite, Vinegar, Mustard, Yeast, Tannin, Bitter, Sharp, Tangy, Sugar, Sweet, Honey, Eggs, Putrid, Pungent, Bland.

## Great Britain

Stilton

Appleby's Cheshire

Berkswell

Montgomery's Cheddar

Golden Cross

# France

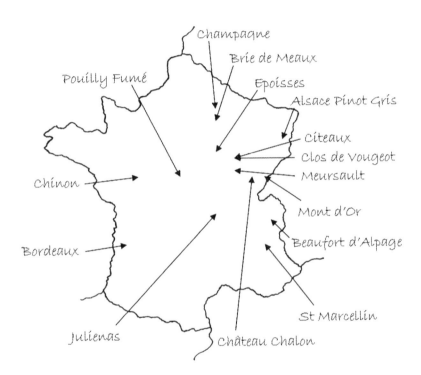

Champagne

Brie de Meaux

Pouilly Fumé

Epoisses

Alsace Pinot Gris

Cîteaux

Clos de Vougeot

Meursault

Chinon

Mont d'Or

Bordeaux

Beaufort d'Alpage

St Marcellin

Julienas

Château Chalon

23

## Italy

Parmigiano Reggiano

## Spain and Portugal

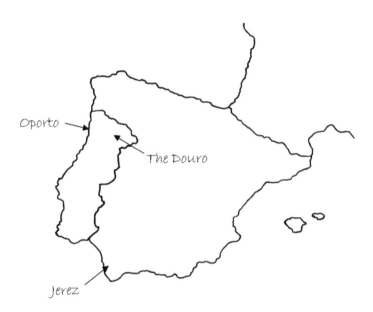

AT THE SIGN OF THE GOLDEN CROSS

## ❖ Golden Cross: Kevin and Alison Blunt

Ten miles inland from Eastbourne, East Sussex, just off the A22, lies the hamlet of Golden Cross. Its name derives from the 19th century inn at the sign of 'The Golden Cross' at that location but, more interestingly, it is the cheese to which it has given its name that, nowadays, sets hearts racing at the mention of Golden Cross. The cheese, quite simply, is superb.

Kevin and Alison Blunt make this gem on their smallholding of 6 acres, which they share with 240 milking goats and 90 kids. They never intended to make cheese, but were persuaded to do so when a neighbour decided to return to his native France and sold them his milking parlour and cheese-making equipment. At the time, in 1989, they were living in a mobile home and literally built everything themselves, including their house! They have three children who have grown up learning to help Mum & Dad with the cheesemaking and looking after the goats. They have not looked back, and now make over 1,000 cheeses each week; not enough to satisfy demand but to increase production would, they feel, risk reducing the quality.

They spend nearly all their waking hours in pursuit of their business, which is also their way of life. Just milking the goats (Saanens, British Alpines and Toggenburgs) takes 5 hours a day and that's before a single cheese is made. The goats all graze outside during the summer and are fed hay all year round. Kevin has split them into three kidding groups to try and provide cheese throughout the year. At peak season, they produce up to 800 litres of milk, which Kevin and Alison then set about making into cheese. To do this, Alison heats the milk to 20°c, and then adds a starter culture, microbial rennet and penicillium. The curd is left in a warm room for 24 hours to form a curd and, the next day, is hand-ladled into tall cylindrical moulds. At the end of the day the cheeses are turned upside down to get an even distribution of moisture. The next morning the cheeses are taken out of their moulds and moved to a drying

29

room, where they are sprinkled with salt and charcoal. The charcoal alters the acidity of the surface of the cheese and aids the maturation, giving the right conditions for the growth of the penicillium mould. Kevin and Alison continue to turn the cheeses daily until they judge that they are ready for despatch to customers.

So, although they do now have some help, it is definitely a full time job!

And what of the finished cheese? Golden Cross has a delightful, velvety bloom on the outside, the result of the penicillium, which Alison adds, and its log shape immediately makes it look interesting and appealing. But it is when the log is cut that the appearance becomes truly stunning because, there revealed is the intense white of the interior, surrounded by a thin black circle of charcoal which, in turn, is coated with the white bloom on the outside. Served on a black charcoal biscuit, it looks spectacular. I also enjoy Golden Cross sliced on top of a salad of grilled Mediterranean vegetables, with the cheese slightly warmed but not melted.

When young, Golden Cross has a fine, firm, silky texture and a fresh, tangy flavour with a hint of lemon. As it ripens, the body of the cheese becomes denser and creamier and the flavour takes on a more complex array of flavours – caramel, lemon, vanilla, grass and a host of others, all in harmony with each other and increasing in intensity with each passing day.

The pleasure of those who eat the cheese is sufficient testament to its quality, but Golden Cross has also won many awards; not least of which was the James Aldridge Trophy for the best unpasteurised British cheese, which The Prince of Wales presented to Kevin and Alison. That was one day which the Blunts had to be persuaded to spend time away from their farm, but even then they had to hurry back to milk the goats.

## ❖ Other top goats' milk cheeses

Goats' cheeses are amongst my favourites. I find something particularly attractive about their fresh, steely, lightly-acidic style, which seems far less cloying, or fatty, than cows' milk cheeses. I also like the intense white colour of their paste, which can be in striking contrast to their rind and makes for a very attractive appearance on the cheeseboard.

Despite these common characteristics, goats' milk cheeses come in almost as many shapes and styles as cows' milk cheeses, and it is a mistake to think of them as all one category. The range of flavours and textures in goats' cheeses runs from extremely mild, fresh young cheeses to some aged cheeses, especially from France, Italy or Spain, which can be fierce, fiery and extremely 'goaty'. France is a land par excellence for 'chèvres', with the Loire valley and the Mediterranean coastline being the predominant regions; but recently there has been something of a renaissance in goats' milk cheesemaking in Britain.

Although goats' cheeses are very well matched to light modern diets, they were, in fact, amongst the earliest cheeses to be made. When Sumerian man was first making cheese some 5,000 years ago, it was almost certainly from the milk of either goats or sheep. This tradition has been preserved all around the Mediterranean although elsewhere, since the Middle Ages, cows have sometimes displaced goats and sheep due to their higher yield.

The smaller fat particles and a unique fatty acid structure make goats' milk cheeses easier to digest than cows' milk cheeses and thus suitable for a wider range of consumers.

Goats' cheeses remain fairly seasonal, with cheesemaking generally taking place from January to October. The reason for this is that the kids are, in the main, born at the beginning of the year, with the does giving milk for some 9

31

months thereafter. The best time to enjoy goats' cheeses, therefore, starts in the spring and runs through to the autumn.

Banon from the south of France is easily identifiable because it is wrapped in a chestnut leaf tied with raffia. It is soft with a, sometimes, sticky rind inside the leaf, and a mild, faintly sour lactic flavour.

There are other cheeses, such as Tommette and Bûchette Sarriette, which are basically the same as Banon but without the chestnut leaf and presented in a variety of shapes and sizes.

I also love Chabichou du Poitou with its crinkled skin, crumbly texture and delicate, slightly sweet flavour reminiscent of nuts and herbs. Shaped like a truncated cone, it is made in the Poitou region of western France and allegedly was introduced by the Moors when they occupied the region in the 8th century.

Crottin de Chavignol is perhaps one of the most well-known French goats cheeses. It is made in and around the village of Chavignol, near Sancerre in the Loire valley, and they are ideal accompaniments to each other. There are four stages of maturation for Crottin de Chavignol: Demi Sec, when it is young, fresh and quite soft; Bleuté which is a when blue moulds are just starting to appear on the surface and the cheese is firmer with a more distinct taste; Bleu when the blue moulds have covered the whole cheese giving it a somewhat dry, powdery flavour; and Repassé which is when the cheese has been kept in earthenware pots for 3-4 weeks and is very strong flavoured.

The other great goats' cheeses from the Loire are Selles Sur Cher, Ste Maure, Pouligny St Pierre and Valençay, all of which I find irresistible. They are different shapes and from different villages but otherwise they all share a similar smooth texture and salty lactic flavour with hints of hazelnuts.

# AT THE SIGN OF THE GOLDEN CROSS

 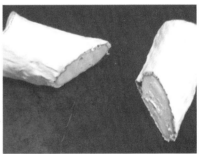

Alison and Kevin Blunt's Golden Cross Cheese

Edward and Chris                    Cheese

# A Chalet In High Alpine Pastures

rt d'Alpage

# PARTNERS ON THE TABLES OF LYON

Etoile de Vercor's St Marcellin

# FRANCE LOSES A WAR: THE WORLD GAINS A CHEESE

Luc and Jean-Michel Donge's Brie de Meaux

Giorgio Cravero's Parmigiano Reggiano

# A WINTER'S TALE

Patrick Richard's Mont d'Or

# A Modern Champion

Stephen Fletcher's Berkswell

# A STINKER FROM DIJON

Jean Berthaut's Epoisses

# THE QUINTESSENTIAL BRITISH CHEESE

Jamie Montgomery's Cheddar

# THE CISTERCIAN'S: CHEESE'S GREAT BENEFACTORS

Fromage de L'Abbaye de Citeaux

# WEARY TRAVELLERS NAME A CHEESE

Stilton

# THE WINES

La Moynerie Pouilly Fume

Thierry Redde

Vincent Bitouzet

Father and Son in the vineyard

Patrice Noyelle

Pol Roger offices

# THE WINES

Lilian and Sandrine Matray

Harvest at Domaine Matray

Francois-Xavier Barc, Domaine Joguet

Francois-Xavier Barc, Domaine Joguet

Juan Garcia Jarana

Dry Oloroso Pata de Gallina

# THE WINES

The village of Chateau Chalon

Jean Berthet-Bondet in his cellar

Fonseca casks for ageing tawny port

Bruce Guimaraens of Fonseca Port

Christian Bas in 1975

Maison Kuentz-Bas

# THE WINES

Vignoble Dourthe Chateau La Garde

Vignoble Dourthe Chateau La Garde

Clos de Vougeot

Philippe Engel

Quinta de Vargellas

Adrian Bridge of Taylor's Port

Cerney, which is made in the Cotswolds, can be regarded as an English version of Valençay because of its shape but, in fact, has a drier texture. It is simply delicious grilled.

Tymsboro is also worth looking out for. Developed by Mary Holbrook at her farm just south west of Bath, it can be sublime but can be a little variable.

Another marvellous English goats milk cheese is Perroche made by Charlie Westhead in Herefordshire. It needs to be eaten very fresh, within a week to 10 days of making, and has the most delicate of flavours. Mousse like in texture, it melts in the mouth.

Of the harder goats cheeses, Ticklemore is one of my favourites, especially when well-matured. It is hard and nutty, with complex herby flavours.

My final selection is Bouton d'Oc, a mini, pear-shaped cheese pierced by a small stick and weighing in at just 15g. With its fine texture and typical mild goaty flavour, it makes an ideal accompaniment to an aperitif.

## ❖ Reflections from the Loire

I arrived in Touraine, the birthplace of many a fine goats' cheese, and Immediately, I felt at home in this delightful region. Manoir de la Remoniere, where I stayed, is a lovely, large 15th century house; somewhat ramshackle and dilapidated outside but my room was delightful, spacious and very comfortable. The manoir stands just across the River Indre from Azay Le Rideau and I could see the Château from the terrace outside my room. The host family were friendly and welcoming. I dined at Les Grottes, which was excellent. My 'amuse-bouche' was superb; melon, tea and mint in a very light frothy cross between a mousse and a drink. After dinner I walked round the Château for their Son et Lumière which was enchanting. My favourite scene was 'The Woods', with rainbow lights dotted in the trees, as if the light had been refracted through a diamond, with 'nature' music and bird calls.

The next morning I visited Leboeuf-Dalonneau, a small farm just outside Ste Maure, making Ste Maure cheese. Their land is used for cereals with their 120 goats kept inside all year and milked where they live (no milking parlour) — what a boring life, never a change of scene. There is a small dairy where they make the cheese — basic and showing signs of ageing but clean enough.

I lunched at Hôtel d'Espagne in Valençay. Slow service but excellent smoked salmon chopped into tiny pieces and bound together by a light sauce (probably fromage frais). Served with the most delicate cream of cucumber; mousse-like. Simply superb.

After lunch I visited Maurice Laville at Fromagerie Hardy in Meusnes. They don't make cheese but buy from farmers when the cheeses are about 3 days old and mature them for 10-15 days. A very efficient operation and clearly passionate about quality in what they do; hygienic, controlled, calm, efficient. They handle Selles sur cher, Ste Maure and Valençay. All are made to exactly the same recipe; it is only the shape of the cheese which differs, although this will affect the maturing of the cheese and hence, slightly, the finished flavour. The making of Pouligny St Pierre differs, in that the curds are pre-drained before putting in the moulds (as with Crottin de Chavignol). This results in a firmer, fuller-bodied cheese with a sturdier flavour. The process is basically: milk into vats; add starter culture; after 2 hours add rennet; leave for 18 hours during which the curds coagulate; then into moulds for 18 hours. The cats' hair grey mould, which sometimes appears on the cheeses in the spring, is linked to the blooming of the trees.

I went on to Fromagerie Jacquin. They are quite a big operation producing 800 tons a year. Like Hardy, they also mature farmhouse cheeses but are not keen to promote them. They pasteurise everything.

A little drive to the east is Sancerre, which I approached from Touraine. I started looking for an hotel when I left Vierzon. Nothing was to be found en-route but I thought there must be a nice hotel in Sancerre itself. There wasn't.

After a terrible night at a not very good and overpriced hotel in Cosne sur Loire, I ventured to Chavignol, just outside Sancerre to visit, after a not bad lunch at 'Au Fin Chavignol', Gilles Dubois. He was late – a bad start. But his operation is good; just like Hardy in Touraine – affineurs not makers. They have a nice shop and functional 'caves'.

In the evening to Château de Maulmont, just outside Vichy. Well advertised; placards all the way along the route. Good reviews in the guides, good food, pleasant atmosphere, but the place has no personal touch, no personality to it. It's all a bit too commercial. Is there a manager? Is there an owner? It runs as a business not as a passion.

## ❖ Pouilly Fumé La Moynerie 2003: Domaine Michel Redde

I should say here that wines made from the Sauvignon grape are not my favourites. I find that, whilst they are refreshing and zesty, they can also be green, acidic, aggressive and reminiscent of unripe fruit.

However, when paired with goats' cheeses both wine and cheese take on new dimensions – the marriage brings out in both hitherto hidden qualities.

Sancerre and Pouilly Fumé are the most fashionable wines made from Sauvignon, but New Zealand and South Africa are rapidly developing their own reputations. I find that New Zealand tends to accentuate the qualities I dislike in Sauvignon, whereas South Africa exhibits many of the qualities I do like but in more muted form and at a lower price than the French. However, for the purposes of matching with goats' cheeses there is no doubt that the Loire valley is the spiritual, as well as physical heartland for Sauvignon. The wines produced here are almost invariably a good match for goats' cheeses; hardly a surprise as, dotted amongst the vineyards, are little farms with a few goats in their barns, from whose milk are produced some of the most sublime goats' cheeses.

Sauvignon is also, of course, an essential ingredient, along with Semillon, in the magnificent sweet wines of Bordeaux, which are such a good match with blue cheeses. But I find the dry wines produced in Bordeaux tend to dullness, lacking the pungency and intensity of wines made further north in the Loire. Californian Sauvignons tend towards a melony flavour which is not so suited to goats' cheese.

To enjoy with goats' cheeses, my money is on Sancerre, Pouilly Fumé and many of the lesser-known Loire wines such as Quincy, Reuilly, Menetou-Salon and even a basic Sauvignon de Touraine. In a good vintage, such wines are refreshing, not too aggressive and possess a flinty, grassy, herbaceous edge to the fruit, with a hint of crushed nettles which is a perfect foil for goats' cheese.

Many years ago Rachel and I visited Michel Redde at his vineyard just north of Pouilly-sur-Loire. We had a fascinating tasting followed by lunch in a local restaurant. I have remembered his wines with fondness ever since and recently his son, Thierry, was kind enough to send me a bottle of his Pouilly Fumé La Moynerie 2003. I couldn't wait to get some goats' cheese to taste with it and, as luck would have it, I had some Golden Cross in prime condition. The two might have been made for each other. The La Moynerie had a lovely nose, gooseberry, as is typical of Sauvignon, but really full and soft with none of the sourness which one can sometimes find. On the palate it was soft, rounded, full, harmonious, elegant and long lasting, with just the right balance of flinty austerity to give the wine some backbone and structure, and to prevent it being soft and floppy. None of the over-austerity found in some Sauvignons. A great wine. The Golden Cross was soft and silky in texture with the rind providing a delightful contrast of texture. The flavour was lemony, grassy and full. The two together complimented each other to perfection.

In 1991, Thierry took charge of the enterprise, becoming the sixth generation of the Redde family to cultivate vines on this vineyard. This allowed Michel to fulfil his childhood dream of painting; he had great success bringing pleasure to many with his paintings, just as he did with his wines.

The 40 hectare vineyard covers some areas of flinty soils and some of limestone chalk. Grapes grown in the flinty areas give a spiciness to the wine while those from limestone areas tend to produce rounder and softer wines. Neither is perfect by itself but Thierry's blending masterfully brings out the best of both. It is one of the secrets that makes the La Moynerie wine so special. Generally he uses about two-thirds from the limestone chalk areas and one-third from the flinty areas; this partially accounts for the wonderful depth of his wines.

I have found other Sauvignons which partner Golden Cross well; sometimes a Sancerre, which can be more flinty, makes an excellent match; but I love the La Moynerie wine and can thoroughly recommend it.

## ❖ Buying cheese: What to look for

For me, and I hope you, cheese is more than mere sustenance. It should provide pleasure in eating, stimulate the senses, and have a sufficiently complex flavour to be interesting. To me, great cheeses should have character, harmony, finesse, layers of flavour, delicacy and complexity; revealing the nuances of their character with every mouthful.

37

To achieve this is no easy task. It demands the skill of the herdsman to produce immaculate raw milk, and the skill of the cheesemaker to turn that milk into a great cheese. At its heart, cheesemaking is basically a simple process and the best cheeses are usually produced in the simplest of ways. What is required is an innate skill, a feel for the milk, almost a sixth sense by which the cheesemaker knows the best thing to do at any point in the process. This cannot be done on a large scale in a factory; it requires the personal surroundings of a small dairy where the cheesemaker is in tune with his, or often her, environment and, above all, where they have the independence to follow their instinct rather than a given set of instructions.

What I find so interesting about cheesemaking is its mix of art and science; science is the base, no good cheese can be made if the science is wrong, the temperature too high, the time taken too long or the milk impure. But equally, no great cheese can be made by science alone; the greatness comes with the art. Factory cheeses can sometimes be good but I have never found them to be great. Their only positives are, perhaps, a uniformity of flavour and a cheaper price. I have found that all the best cheeses are produced by small artisan producers, often using the milk from a single herd, and almost always using unpasteurised milk. Artisan making alone is not a guarantee of quality, but it is an essential place to start if you are looking for great cheese. For me, the charm of a hand-made cheese, preserving the flavours provided by nature, always trumps anything mass-produced. Perhaps the nature of specialist cheeses is best summed up by a cheesemaker who said "We feel blessed that we make a living doing what we love, not maximising profit for shareholders"

I really recommend that you find a specialist cheese shop from which to buy your cheese. If you cannot find one near you, look for a good delicatessen or independent food shop, farm shop or farmers' market. If, and only if, you can't discover one of those (and I'll find that hard to believe) should you consider buying cheese from a supermarket.

So what should you look for when you visit the shop? For me, the signs of a good cheese shop are:

- Fantastic quality cheeses (obviously!)
- The cheeses are well cared for
- They stock interesting and unusual cheeses
- A good range of artisan-produced cheeses
- Cheeses are cut to order, not pre-cut
- They offer the opportunity to taste in the shop
- Staff who know their cheeses and can advise on the style and ripeness of each one
- Good, clean and hygienic conditions
- A pleasant atmosphere in which to shop
- A limited range of great cheeses is much better than a huge range of poor cheeses

You should be able to rely on such a shop to sell you first class cheeses in good condition, but it is worth checking. Other customers may have different views, and the perfect cheese is a very subjective matter. A good start is to ask a few questions:

- Is it produced by traditional methods
- Is it small, artisan human scale production
- Is it made by a cheesemaker of proven ability
- Is it naturally produced, or organic
- Is it unpasteurised
- Is it made from the fresh milk of a single herd
- Is it appellation contrôlée / PDO / DO or other quality mark
- Can the shop tell you about the maker / have they been there

The answer to all these questions should be a resounding YES

Then ask the shop for a taste; good shops will be only too pleased to offer a taste of any cheese they are cutting, but probably not small whole cheeses. If you meet with resistance, go elsewhere.

If you're not in the mood for tasting, examine the cheeses. Unfortunately there is no sure way of judging the quality of a cheese simply by looking at it, or its packaging, but there are a few signs which indicate to me that a cheese is likely to be of poor quality:

- Wrapped in thick plastic or vacuum packed
- Cracked or dried-out rinds
- Physical deformities, bulging or collapsing
- Wet or damp rinds on cheeses which should be dry, giving a soggy texture
- Brown or black mould - most other moulds are nothing to worry about
- Wrappers stuck to the cheese
- Soft cheeses which are heavy-textured or hardened
- Blotchy or discoloured interiors
- Putrid or ammonia smell which persists more than about 10 minutes
- Sour or excessively bitter taste
- Excessively strong or aggressive taste
- Overly vegetal taste
- Off or unclean flavours

When buying cheese, most people choose a variety of different tastes and textures (e.g. one hard, one soft, one blue and one goat); that always proves popular because there is generally something for everyone. An interesting alternative is to choose several cheeses which are similar to each other (e.g. three different sheep's cheeses), or for something really special choose just one stunning cheese (e.g. a large hunk of 3-year-old Parmigiano Reggiano or a whole Mont d'Or).

If you're going for variety, the two most important considerations are: texture (hard or soft) and strength of flavour (strong or mild). Armed with a decision on these two critical factors, you will find your choice of cheese much easier.

In choosing your cheeses, you could also take account of the type of milk, region of production, the rind, or whether it is a blue cheese.

Whichever route you choose, try not to have lots of small pieces of cheese. I find it much more attractive to have larger pieces of fewer varieties. In any case, small pieces of cheese dry up much quicker than larger pieces; which means that you may end up with more to throw away.

Your choice of cheese should also be influenced by what other foods you will be serving. For instance, if you are serving a very full-flavoured main course it will be hard to taste very mild cheeses afterwards.

The quantity you will need is often hard to judge. It will depend on the type of occasion, how much other food you are serving and how many of your guests enjoy cheese. As a rough guide I generally allow:

|  | Canapé | Main course | Cheeseboard |
| --- | --- | --- | --- |
| 1 cheese | 75g | 175g | 75g |
| 3 or 4 cheeses | 25g | 60g | 25g |
| More than 5 cheeses | 15g | 35g | 15g |

All weights are per person per cheese. They are only a rough guide. Only you will know, through experience, how much your friends are likely to eat.

Cheese starts deteriorating as soon as it is cut into, so bear in mind that it is better to buy little-and-often than to stock up.

## ❖ Serving Cheese

It is essential to bring cheeses to room temperature (about 20°c) an hour or two before serving.

Arrange the cheeses on a cheeseboard: marble, wood with an attractive grain; terracotta or glass are all good materials for a cheeseboard. I prefer a plain cheeseboard, but decorate it if you like. Bay leaves & tangerines, soft summer fruits & fresh herbs, dried fruits and walnuts, dandelion & nasturtium leaves, or flowers all make attractive displays.

Personally I enjoy eating cheese simply by itself with a knife and fork, but many people enjoy bread, biscuits or other accompaniments. Bread and cheese has been a classic throughout history – a hearty chunk of bread and cheese being the classic ploughman's. You can serve French bread, Wholemeal, Rye, Nut or Olive breads – whichever you prefer. Biscuits provide a contrast of textures, which some people like, although I am not too keen on them.

To me butter is unnecessary with all but the driest cheeses but, if you do serve butter, try to make it unsalted as most cheeses already contain some salt. Celery, raw carrots, water cress, apples and other crudités provide a good means of cleansing the palate if a number of different cheeses are to be eaten, or if cheese is the main course of a meal.

Pickles, chutneys and other vinegar based accompaniments are a pet hate of mine but, I know, give pleasure to others. Walnuts are a delight with many blue cheeses, as is quince paste with sheep's cheeses and honey or fresh pears with Parmigiano Reggiano.

One of the most surprising combinations I found to work was Mandarin Marmalade and Celtic Promise (a firm washed rind cheese). You can experiment with other combinations specific to various cheeses, but ideally do not choose an accompaniment with too much flavour, as it will mask the flavours of the cheeses. The choice is yours but don't feel obliged to overdo it; good cheese by itself, eaten with a knife and fork is more than enough.

As well as a cheeseboard you need some good knives; a sturdy knife for hard cheeses and one with holes in the blade for soft cheeses. Ideally you will use a different knife for different types of cheese, in order to avoid transferring the flavour of one type to another. For this purpose you can consider there to be five types of cheese: Fresh, Bloomy rind, Washed rind, Hard and Blue. A cheese wire is useful for cutting larger pieces of hard cheese as it gives a good clean cut.

I find that my guests often ask what the cheeses are. If there are more than 4 or 5, a verbal explanation is soon forgotten so it is helpful to put a little label on or beside the cheese. The label can show as much or as little information as you like, but I find it useful to show at least the name of the cheese and the suggested order in which they should be eaten. Number them starting at 1, mildest first, strongest last.

As with any food, if you really want to enjoy everything a cheese has to offer, you must take it slowly. Do not rush a cheese tasting. You must concentrate on it as well; it is all too easy to be swept away by conversation and miss many of the finer points of a cheese.

For both cheese and wine, I find there are four aspects to consider: appearance, aroma, texture (even wine has a texture or mouth feel) and taste. All four need to be appealing for a cheese or wine to be great. All four are subjective. Your opinion may differ from mine. It doesn't matter. In fact that is part of the interest.

When to serve your cheese never fails to divide opinions; before or after dessert? I find the ideal flow of flavours is Main Course – Salad – Cheese – Dessert. The purpose of the salad is to refresh the palate ready for the cheese, and probably means you will eat less cheese. Also, the wine you serve with the main course can usually do service to the cheese as well. The major reason for not serving cheese after dessert is that I find cheese doesn't taste very good after something sweet. I accept that it is a personal opinion and in our house we serve cheese and dessert at the same time, allowing guests to choose which to have first.

A Farmhouse In The North Of England

## ❖ Mrs Appleby's Cheshire

"Where's the cheese room?" I asked as I sat in the 18th century farmhouse kitchen with Edward and Christine Appleby and Edward's parents Lance and Lucy. "Just across the hall. The dining room's on the left, the cheese room's on the right" said Lucy. Her reply has stayed with me, because it shows just how integral cheese is to both this family and this farm.

Hawkestone Abbey Farm sits at the edge of the Cheshire Plain, formed by the River Dee. The area provides lush fertile grazing and has long been noted for its dairy farming. Indeed, Cheshire is the oldest recorded English cheese. Certainly it was mentioned in The Domesday Book; it is also said to have been one of the Celtic cheeses already being made in Britain when the Romans came, and there is some evidence that it was even taken to Rome by the legions. The Romans mined salt in the area and it is hard to avoid the conclusion that the salt deposits under the pastures on which the cows graze are responsible, at least in part, for the character of the cheese. Not that Cheshire cheese tastes more salty than others – it has less than half the salt of Feta – but its fresh character somehow brings to mind fresh sea breezes and the tang of salt on the face.

Over the years, Cheshire cheese's popularity increased until it became far and away Britain's most widely eaten cheese in the 19th century, easily outselling Cheddar. So much so that whole 'cheese trains' took the cheese from Cheshire to London. The 1920's saw over 1,000 farms making Cheshire cheese. The Second World War, which affected all British cheesemaking, had a particularly dire effect in Cheshire. Post war, Cheshire cheese fell out of popularity partly because, being crumbly, it was difficult to pre-pack; partly because a cheese grader called Groves liked thin acidic cheeses, a taste not shared by the public; partly because farmers were slow to start making cheese again as it was far easier to sell their milk as liquid to the Milk Marketing Board; and partly because factory production, which took over, produced bland anonymous cheese, giving all Cheshire cheese an undeserved poor reputation. Today there is but a handful of farms producing Cheshire cheese, with Appleby's being the only one using traditional methods and raw milk from the farm.

It was in this depressing post war state that Lucy found herself when she married Lance Appleby. Lucy was from a farming family and had made cheese all her life, so it was natural she should take responsibility for cheesemaking at Hawkestone when they started in 1952. She had a flair for it. Even when not making cheese, simply walking through the cheese room, she could tell if something was wrong. She would have a 'feeling' that, say, the temperature was too high and nine times out of ten she would be right. And this is why the proximity of the cheese room to the house was so important. Even when doing something else, she could keep an eye on the cheese.

When they started, Lance and Lucy were operating in a highly regulated environment with the Milk Marketing Board having exclusive rights to sell their cheese. It was not an environment that encouraged individuality or, one might say, excellence. Once they had made the cheese, the Appleby's lost sight of it, not knowing where it was sold, to whom, in what quantities or even if the customer liked it or not. The result was that Cheshire cheese became more and more bland, often indistinguishable from Wensleydale, Lancashire or Caerphilly. Indeed some unscrupulous dairies made just one cheese and put on whichever label the customer had ordered!

In contrast, the Appleby's worked away at producing the best cheeses they could; although with little reward for their labours. It was not until the early 1980's that Lance and Lucy were allowed to sell their cheese directly to customers. They jumped at it, and soon the excellence of Lucy's cheesemaking ensured a demand specifically for her cheese. Almost without knowing it, she was creating a brand.

Time has moved on and Lucy no longer makes the cheese. That important job falls to Gary Gray who has been at it a number of years now. Production has grown to 80 tonnes a year, all made from the unpasteurised milk of their own herd of nearly 300 Friesians, which are milked twice a day, at 5am and 3pm, in a state-of-the art rotary milking parlour.

The process Gary follows, making cheese, is more or less unchanged from that used by Lucy Appleby. He heats the milk in the large open-topped vat to 30°c and adds a live starter culture. One change, however, is in the rennet. He now uses a vegetarian rennet substitute, which he feels makes little difference to the cheese but widens the market to include vegetarians. The curds form and are then cut so as to release the whey. The vat is heated to expel even more whey. Gary adds a little salt and the curds are then milled and put into calico lined cylindrical moulds. The newly-made cheeses are then pressed for 24 to 48 hours, then removed from their moulds and wrapped in a fresh calico cloth. Ageing begins on the farm, where they are rubbed and turned every day for a minimum of 6 weeks, and often longer.

The right age at which to eat Appleby's Cheshire is a hotly disputed topic. I like it at about 4 months of age but others prefer it at 6 months or more, when it has developed more flavour. But to me, although the flavour has intensified, it looses its lively, fresh flavours with their hints of citrus and sea spray. Appleby's Cheshire never shouts its flavours from the rooftops. It is simply and quietly a lovely cheese. It has great depth of flavour, which is not to be confused with strength of flavour. Its flavours are delicate, almost elusive but they last in the mouth – a long, lingering, delightful reminder of a summer's day. Savoury, herby, lactic, citrusy are all words you could use to describe this special cheese. And that's before you consider the texture of the cheese; moist, light, flaky, crumbly, it almost falls apart in your hands.

Finally, its colour. It can be red, white or blue. Naturally it is white, but the more usual version nowadays is red (or more precisely a delicate shade of salmon), which is achieved by adding annatto to the milk in the vat. Originally it was carrot juice, which was added purely for visual effect, with no discernable change in the taste.

Blue Cheshire is a relative rarity, but all Cheshires have a tendency to blue naturally due to their open, crumbly texture which allows the blue mould to take hold. I have heard customers reject it as 'mouldy cheese' but others consider it a delicacy. With cheese everyone has his or her own opinion.

I like Appleby's Cheshire by itself, or perhaps with an apple, but it also makes a superb Welsh Rarebit, grilled gently. I don't go for any fancy recipe; for me a slice of buttered toast, topped with plenty of cheese and grilled until bubbling is a wonderful snack, especially on cold days.

### ❖ Other delightful crumbly cheeses

Another member of the 'crumbly' family of cheeses is Lancashire. Its supreme maker is Ruth Kirkham. I have known and loved her cheese for many years. She, her husband John, and son Graham, have a small farm at Goosnargh just outside Preston. John milks the cows; Ruth and Graham make the cheese every day of the year - including Christmas Day, New Year's Day, Easter Day, birthdays and every other kind of day. Apparently the first time Ruth went on a train was in 1989 when she went to London – ostensibly to receive a prize for her cheese but she spent most of the time shopping in Oxford Street. Anyway the cheese is great. Each day she keeps back some of the curd and mixes the curd from 4 different days milkings into each cheese. So a cheese she makes today will have ¼ today's curd, ¼ yesterday's, ¼ the day before and ¼ the day before that. It's pretty unique. The cheese is crumbly yet really creamy with a lactic tang. By producing such good cheese and sticking to raw milk when others were pasteurising, they built up such a good trade that they were able to buy the farm they had previously held as tenants; a lovely success story.

Wensleydale is the third of the great crumbly cheeses from the north of England and probably the original. Monks accompanying William the Conqueror in 1066 brought with them the recipe from France, and it is thought that this was for a cheese akin to Roquefort. Thus Wensleydale started life as a blue cheese made from sheep's milk. Over the years, most likely after the dissolution of the monasteries, it became a cows' milk cheese and lost its blue. Nowadays good Wensleydale is hard to come by. The best maker is Suzanne Stirke but Hawes Dairy cheeses can be good too.

Caerphilly completes the line-up of great British crumblies and is a relatively recent invention, having first been made for Welsh miners in the 19th century. Designed as a cheese to be eaten young, it is a cheese with easy appeal but the best, such as Gorwydd, can also be aged a few months with good results. They become, in effect, totally different cheeses with more complex flavours. Because it matured quickly, Caerphilly was of great interest to cheddar makers and thus it was that Somerset became the main area for the production of Caerphilly. One happy result of this was the emergence in the 1980's of Chris Duckett as the prime maker of fine Caerphilly.

Alongside his Caerphilly he produces a similar cheese with a thin sprinkling of chives in the middle, which he calls Wedmore after his local village.

One of the earliest cheeses to emerge in the renaissance of British cheesemaking in the 1980's was Yarg, which was the makers name — Gray — spelled backwards. Covered in nettle leaves, it has a distinctive appearance and although the flavour is mild, it is nonetheless a very pleasant cheese with easy appeal.

A cheese similar to Cheshire, but made in West Wales, is Llangloffan, made by

Leon Downey. He is an interesting man who used to be Lead Viola with the Hallé Orchestra. His cheese is superb; often giving Appleby's Cheshire a run for its money.

## ❖ Meursault Clos du Cromin 2003: Domaine Bitouzet-Prieur

The 15th century church of St Nicholas dominates the village of Meursault, just south of Beaune in Burgundy, but it is the vineyards that surround it which have given Meursault its everlasting fame and made it one of my favourite white Burgundies. Although a little red wine is produced in the village, the vignerons long ago decided that Chardonnay was the grape to grow, because the white marl soil amidst chalk is particularly favourable for Chardonnay. The gently undulating vineyards, which extend to some 420 hectares, entitled to the Meursault name, are mainly east facing giving them good exposure to the sun, and vary in height between 230 and 360 metres above sea level.

The wines produced in this small area can be amongst the finest known to man; reaching sublime perfection. They can also be disappointing, either because they are too young or because a grower has more interest in capitalising on Meursault's reputation than living up to it.

Meursault, like most fine White Burgundies, is a delight with many dishes; in my view particularly with smoked salmon. Although it can be tricky with cheese, as the cheese may overpower the wine, with a good Cheshire, such as Appleby's, it can be an admirable partner but; as everywhere in Burgundy, buying from the right grower is essential.

Fortunately there are quite a few, ranging in excellence and price. My favourite, for a good balance of price and excellence, is Domaine Bitouzet-Prieur. In a number of tastings it has come out consistently well. A little more expensive than the cheapest, it is also considerably cheaper, and often better, than the most expensive.

Vincent Bitouzet is the current generation of this family of vine growers; overseeing the production from 12 hectares of vines in Meursault and the next village of Volnay, where barrels and bottles of wine gently mature in ancient cellars underneath his house. Vincent's family have tended the vines and made wine here for over 200 years and, from the start, were keen to bottle their own wines rather than sell in bulk to a wine merchant. This proved a wise move, with Vincent's grandfather winning awards for his wines as long ago as 1860.

Vincent is married to Annie Prieur, whose family are also respected vignerons and part of their vineyards are now looked after by Vincent and their son, Francois.

When I tasted Vincent's 2003 vintage Clos du Cromin, from a one hectare walled parcel of vines to the north east of the village, in 2006 it was a delight with Appleby's Cheshire. Pale gold with flashes of green. A fine floral, slightly smokey, honeysuckle bouquet. On the palate it was very elegant with soft fruit somewhere between white peach and citrus, some vanilla, slightly toasty, hazelnuts and honey playing second fiddle behind a certain richness, balanced by just the right acidity. Delicious now, but hinting at even greater things to come. Classic Meursault. Probably not as long a keeper as some vintages, and at its best in another 4 or 5 years.

2003 was noted for a heat-wave during the summer and Vincent had completed the harvest, exceptionally early, by the end of August. He picks entirely by hand to get the best results and immediately presses the grapes. Vincent believes it is important to ferment the must in small barrels at a cool temperature, which allows extensive contact between wine and lees, resulting in greater richness and complexity in the wine. He allows the wines at least 15 months in cask before bottling.

For a less expensive match, you could try Jean-Luc Terrier's St Veran Domaine des Deux Roches 2003. The domaine is in the village of Davaye, some 8kms west of Macon, and Jean-Luc runs it with Christian Collovray. The two were at school together, became firm friends and even married two sisters, before deciding to work together and establish the domaine in 1985. The wine is fresh and quite appley and is outstanding value for money.

Patrick Javillier, widely regarded as one of Meursault's best growers, is a fan of Meursault with goats' cheeses and blue cheeses but I don't share this passion. His wines can be quite austere, especially when young, with highish acidity indicating that they need considerable time to mature. Rather than complementing the Cheshire, the acidity tends to fight against the cheese and it was not an ideal match. Faiveley's Meursault on the other hand was a good match but lacked the real character and wow factor of Vincent's wine.

## ❖ Seasonal Cheeseboards

Many cheeses used only to be made in certain seasons, following the breeding cycles of the animals. Some still are but most cheeses are now available all year round. Nevertheless it still makes sense to eat certain cheeses at certain times of the year, either because they are actually better at that time of year, or they are suited to a particular season for other reasons. Here are my suggestions:

*Spring*
Goats' milk cheeses are made from roughly January to October and so it is generally late spring (March/April) before the new season's goats' cheeses are available. When they arrive, I always get a lift to my sprits as winter clears away, the days get longer and brighter and I tuck into the lighter, more delicate flavours of fresh goats' cheeses. Sometimes I like to have a cheeseboard composed entirely of goats' cheeses – such as Banon, Valençay, Ticklemore and Golden Cross. Other cheeses to enjoy in the spring are the lighter-

flavoured hard cheeses such as Single Gloucester and such delights as Daylesford Organic, a simply superb cheddar-style cheese bursting with the herby flavours of the pastures. Excellent too are the small soft cheeses, such as St Marcellin, made in the foothills of the alps.

## Summer

With the warmer days of summer, again I am looking for lighter flavours but perhaps something with a little more of the roundness and creaminess one gets from cows' cheeses. This is the season for crumbly cheeses such as Cheshire, Caerphilly and Lancashire. Salads feature prominently in my summer diet and cheeses such as Parmigiano Reggiano, Feta and Mozzarella di Bufala are perfect ingredients. Also, goats' cheeses can still be lovely at this time of year and are especially suitable for picnics, due to their predominantly small size. e.g. Crottin de Chavignol, Ste Maure

## Autumn

As the nights draw in and there's a chill in the air, I find I am looking for stronger flavours and more substantial cheeses. Mimolette is a star at this time of the year, nibbled with a glass of sherry or Madeira as a mid morning snack. Other favourites at this time of year are Berkswell, Double Gloucester (preferably from Jonathan Crump), Brie de Meaux and other soft cheeses such as Waterloo. Some French blue cheeses like Fourme d'Ambert and, of course, Roquefort also eat well in Autumn.

## Winter

With the prospect of some crisp, clear, bright days, a whole new dimension is brought to cheese enjoyment. Such days require cheeses with plenty of flavour and strength - full and robust. Stilton is, of course, a favourite in the winter and a good extra mature Cheddar is also delicious. For the really crisp days there is nothing like some alpine cheeses such as Beaufort, Comté, Raclette and the sublime Mont d'Or, to bring on a feeling of well-being which I normally associate with alpine skiing villages. Washed rind cheeses also seem to come into their own at this time of year; e.g. Livarot, Pont L'Evêque and Epoisses and their English counterparts, Tornegus and Stinking Bishop.

A Chalet In High Alpine Pastures

## ❖ Beaufort d'Alpage: Jean Poccard

Few cheeses demonstrate better than Beaufort the pure and natural simplicity that is at the heart of all cheeses. High in the French Alps, cows graze pastures rich with wild flowers and myriad species of grass, to provide the wonderful summer milk. The breeds are local: Tarine, with their beautiful, chestnut colour and almond eyes and Abondance, easily identifiable with their white faces and rich brown-red bodies. In mountain chalets, alpagistes, such as Jean Poccard, turn their milk into sublime cheeses with immensely complex flavours. Jean's chalet d'alpage is at the end of a 5 km dirt track, which winds its way precariously up the steep gradient of the alp above Peisey-Nancroix, to an altitude of 2,100 metres. The track is made more for animals than modern cars and it was an exciting adventure to approach his chalet in a Citroen C3! The peaks of the Alps ahead, still covered with the remains of last winter's snow, even in September, were a reminder that, in winter, these slopes are a skiers paradise. These same peaks were our guiding star through the first part of the trail where trees encroached on all sides and there were no signs of any grazing. Then the terrain opened out, and we were surrounded by pastures and the gentle tinkle of bells round the necks of cows grazing contentedly in the pure mountain air. And there we came across Jean's chalet, Les Rossets.

In the traditional manner known as 'transhumance', Jean keeps his 160 cows in the valley over winter and makes cheese at his dairy in Peisey-Nancroix but, as summer arrives, he starts moving them up the mountain, grazing adjacent pastures day by day, eventually reaching the foot of the glaciers at 2,600 metres in late July; then returning down the mountain by mid-October. This allows him to make hay from the lower pastures with which to feed his cows in the winter and the cows enjoy the wonderful high alpine pastures during summer. He has two chalets d'alpage where he not only makes the summer cheeses but lives in basic yet cosy accommodation. Other alpagistes will winter their cows in a valley some distance from the summer alpine grazing. I visited one such farmer in the Swiss Jura who moves his cows 'on the hoof' 25 km; taking him seven hours.

Generally Jean has sufficient milk to make two cheeses every morning and two cheeses every evening. Part of the alpage regulations is that Beaufort must be made with milk unpasteurised and fresh from the cows. So they are milked with mobile milking machines in the pastures, and the milk is poured into a simple copper vat which is heated with a naked flame. Jean adds rennet and the curds form. These are ladled into moulds and pressed overnight. The fresh wheels emerge, glistening ivory in colour, from the press and are immersed in brine for a few days and then taken down the mountain to maturing cellars at Aime for affinage.

Quietly nestling in the serenity of the affinage cellars are 9,000 wheels of Beaufort from independent cheesemakers throughout the Tarentaise valley. Each huge cheese, weighing as much as 40kgs, sits in row upon row of wooden shelves, proudly bearing its green Beaufort identification markings, with an additional, special, red marking for alpage cheeses. For the first five months of their lives at Aime, the cheeses are brushed with dry salt twice every week. Thereafter brine replaces the dry salt until the cheeses are ready for sale.

Cheeses made in the valley dairies are turned by machine but the alpage cheeses are turned by hand with loving care, better to cope with their individual characters. Here, Patrice guided me through last summer's cheeses and I was able finally to taste Jean's cheeses. Over a year old, they were simply delicious; rounded, rich, savoury and fruity with hints of hazelnuts; sweetly floral with higher notes of flavour and a lightness and elegance rarely found in other alpine cheeses. Great cheeses indeed.

From time immemorial until the 1960's, the Savoie region was extremely remote and alpage cheesemaking was the norm. Nowadays the valleys of

Beaufortain, Tarentaise and Maurienne are better known for their ski resorts: Courchevel, Val d'Isère, Les Arcs, La Plagne. The building of these resorts opened access to the higher mountain slopes and enabled the milk to be brought down daily into the valleys, where cooperative dairies were built. Jean Poccard is one of only some 15 cheesemakers who still make Beaufort in the traditional alpage way. He fears that his craft is dying out and that soon all cheese will be made in the valleys at dairies like the Cooperative at Beaufort-sur-Doron, which turns out 25,000 cheeses every year and employs 40 people. The milk from 150 farms scattered over the hills arrives here in churns throughout the year and they make some excellent cheese. The Beaufort d'Eté, made with summer milk between June and September, is generally the best with nice high notes but lacking the real complexity of alpage cheeses.

If you want to make a cheese fondue, there is no better cheese than Beaufort mixed with Emmental, but when visiting the region I really enjoy their 'Assiettes Savoyardes', which consist of thinly sliced Beaufort with some Savoyarde charcuterie, bread and a little salad. The Savoie region produces some delicious charcuterie: its own air-dried ham, saucissons made from pork, goat, ass or wild boar; some of which are smoked or have herbs added.

In the modern world, it is easy to forget the essential simplicity of the idea that first motivated man to make cheese; but visiting an alpine chalet like Jean's vividly demonstrates that cheese is essentially a simple means of preserving wonderful summer milk to see one through the harsh winter months. The process need not be complicated and, with milk so pure and rich as that from these high, clear pastures, the resulting cheeses are as stunning as any you will find.

## ❖ Some Other Special Mountain Cheeses

Throughout the Alps, each separate valley seems to produce its own version of what is pretty much the same style of cheese; large cheeses of 40 to 80kgs, hard and dense with an ivory to yellow paste, and a rind reminiscent of leather. To eat them, even in mid-winter, with their floral bouquet and fruity, nutty flavour, is to transport me to the beautiful open spaces and flower-strewn grazing of the high mountain pastures on a warm summer's day.

Comté ranks as the most popular AOC cheese in France because it is widely used in so many types of dishes. Much is of average to good quality but the best cheeses are stunning and are really wasted in recipes. Comté is made in the Jura Mountains of France, close to the Swiss border. One of the most amazing cheese stores I have visited is the Fort des Rousses, which is an old military fort, built in 1882, that has been home to 65,000 wheels of Comté cheese belonging to Marcel Petite since he moved there in 1965. The cool, dark and damp fort is just perfect for maturing cheeses. To me a good Comté is fruity and nutty at the same time, with really complex flavours.

The ubiquitous 'Swiss Cheese' is of course Emmental. So much is this cheese associated with Switzerland that, in the States, they refer to all cheese with holes as 'Swiss Cheese'; so you get Norwegian Swiss, German Swiss and even Swiss Swiss! The holes result from propionic acid gas given off during fermentation, which becomes trapped in the curd. The flavour is nutty and slightly tannic. Look out for 'Cave Aged' Emmental which are the best cheeses but overall it is not one of my favourite cheeses. The flavour is pleasant but I find the texture almost rubbery. These are some of the largest mountain cheeses, weighing in at about 80 kg. 90 cm diameter, 25 cm high.

Good Gruyères, especially those entitled to the 'reserve' label, can be tremendous but all too often I find Gruyère undistinguished, though seldom bad. They have a tantalising herbaceousness overlying a deep nutty flavour. The small, hill-top town of Gruyère is a special place to visit. It is quite touristy, with souvenir shops every few metres, but nonetheless maintains a certain medieval charm.

## ❖ A Champagne moment: Pol Roger 1998

I don't think I have ever refused a glass of Champagne. But that is as nothing compared to Madame Bollinger who famously said:

"I drink my Champagne when I'm happy and when I'm sad.
Sometimes I drink it when I'm alone.
When I have company I consider it obligatory.
I trifle with it if I'm not hungry, and drink it when I am.
Otherwise I never touch it - unless I'm thirsty."

She might have added that it is a mighty fine accompaniment to Beaufort, but the moment and the Champagne has to be right, as I have discovered at a number of tastings. Of course alpine cheeses like Beaufort go well with the local wines, especially whites such as Apremont from Savoie and Fendant from Switzerland (Aigle Les Murailles is a good example). However, I prefer a full-bodied Champagne and this was admirably borne out at a very special tasting which I conducted with Remi Krug, the energetic man behind the Champagne which bears his name. I have to say I was somewhat apprehensive about doing the tasting because I felt that the Champagne might, all too easily, be overpowered by the cheeses and that the tasting would be a disaster. I need not have worried. Although some of the combinations did not work, the sense of adventure and the discovery of some truly superb combinations kept everyone enthralled and we all learned some interesting lessons. It was surprising, for instance, to find that some powerful, mature cheeses were perfect partners for Champagnes.

The best match of all was a Beaufort d'Eté, which went superbly with all the Krug Champagnes. Other good matches were Maroilles with Krug Grande Cuvée, Berkswell with Krug 1989 Vintage and Chaource with Krug Clos du Mesnil 1989.

And the main conclusion? That we are all too confined by the convention that cheese should be served at the end of the meal. Bring the Beaufort to the start of the meal and serve it with a full-bodied Champagne as an appetiser. The moment will be right and, if your guests are half as appreciative as those at my tasting, you will have a success on your hands.

In 1975 I went to work in the Champagne region, where I stayed in a small room above a café and worked for Marne et Champagne, the producers of our Giesler Champagne. I spent some time in all departments of the company: bottling line, blending, packaging etc. and learned quite a lot about the production of Champagne, if not so much about the growing of the grapes. I had little contact with the owner of the business, a somewhat austere man called Monsieur Burtin with looks like General de Gaulle, but towards the end of my stay the sales Director, a lovely man by the name of Monsieur Herriot, invited me to dinner with a colleague. We went to Les Berceaux, an extremely good restaurant in the centre of Epernay where Monsieur Herriot, who knew the simple lodgings I was in, explained to his colleague that they had just spent more on the starter at Les Berceaux than I was spending on a whole week at my café!

The Champagne region of France is one of the most northerly locations where one can expect grapes to have any chance of ripening sufficiently to make a half-reasonable wine. What makes Champagne great rather than half-reasonable is the fact that it is blended and that it is sparkling — the still white wines of Champagne are not up to much.

The bubbles are due to the skills shown, towards the end of the 17th century, by the monks of the Benedictine Abbey of Hautvillers and, in particular, by Dom Pérignon. He discovered that the natural sparkle, which resulted from fermentation, could be trapped in the bottle by using a tight fitting cork and a strong bottle, giving the wine those magnificent bubbles. The process remained a little hit-and-miss until the 19th century when a Monsieur François discovered that a stronger fermentation in bottle could be encouraged by the addition of sugar and yeast; a process perfected by Louis Pasteur. However, fermentation in the bottle produced sediment in the bottle. To cope with this, the wine was sometimes decanted into a fresh bottle or else just sold with the sediment. However, it was not long before the chef des caves at Veuve Clicquot worked out that he could get the sediment into the neck of the bottle by gently shaking and inverting the bottle, a process known as remuage. From there it was a short step to using the pressure in the bottle to expel the sediment when the cork was removed (dégorgement). He topped up the bottle with a little extra wine, re-corked it and the 'Champagne Method' was born. To this day every bottle of Champagne is produced in this way.

Integral to the quality of Champagne is the art of blending wines from different vineyards to produce a wine better than any of its single components. The overall Champagne vineyard area is huge and each of the three main areas – Montagne de Reims, Côte des Blancs and Vallée de la Marne – produces wines quite distinct in style.

Equally big differences result from the different grape varieties: Pinot Noir, Pinot Meunier and Chardonnay. To me Pinot Noir, the historically traditional grape of Champagne, is the foundation of all great Champagnes, giving body, structure, intensity and good ageing potential. A high percentage of Pinot Noir is essential if the Champagne is to be enjoyed with food, especially with cheese. Pinot Meunier is useful in providing fruit and a certain youthful characteristic but is, to my mind, the least valuable of the Champagne grapes. Chardonnay, a relative newcomer to Champagne, is valuable in lightening a little the Pinot Noir and providing a welcome freshness, finesse and elegance. By itself Chardonnay can produce a pleasant aperitif Champagne.

Because of this element of blending, the great wines of Champagne come from businesses known as Champagne Houses, which usually buy in grapes from growers in many different areas to make their wine. The concept of 'Château bottled' is alien to Champagne. The key is not the vineyard or Château but the skill of each Champagne House, in blending. The great blenders are Krug, Bollinger, Ruinart, Louis Roederer, Laurent Perrier, Taittinger, Perrier-Jouet and Pol Roger.

It was to Pol Roger that I made my way one sunny spring day to meet Patrice Noyelle, their very friendly Président du Directoire and the first in the history of the business to be appointed from outside the family. Patrice is from Burgundy, where he still has a house, and was head-hunted from Mommessin when Pol Roger were looking for someone to oversee the transition between generations of the family. He has achieved great things in the eight years he has been at the helm; dusting off some of the old ways and injecting a new sense of purpose and quality into this respected house. Pol Roger remains quite a small house, selling some one and a half million bottles a year compared to Bollinger's three million. Just over half the wine comes from their own 85 hectares of vineyards and just under half is bought in as grapes with Pol Roger overseeing the vinification.

Approaching Pol Roger along the Avenue de Champagne, with its magnificent mansion facades acting as a role call of the famous Champagne houses, it is clear that the Champenois do things in the grand style. The buildings inspire a sense of wonder that a mere wine can generate so much wealth. But Champagne, of course, is not a mere wine. For two centuries it has been revered as an essential part of virtually any celebration. Pol Roger's cellars are at number 34 but it was to their grand offices in a mansion built by the original Pol Roger at the end of the 19th century, that I went to be welcomed in a beautiful salon by Patrice. Style and Champagne are synonymous and Pol Roger has style in spades. It is one of very few Champagne houses to remain under family control – despite Patrice's appointment. He may have been able to persuade the family to part with €1.5 million to improve the cellars but his attempt to cut down a tree in the garden met with severe resistance. A keen gardener, all Patrice wanted to do was create a view of the vineyards from the offices.

Reims may be the historic centre of Champagne and provide part of the reason for Champagne's fame, thanks to most of the French kings being anointed in Reims cathedral, but I can't help thinking of Epernay as the spiritual centre of Champagne. Epernay is surrounded by a gently rolling countryside scattered with vineyards, a good view of which is now afforded from Pol Roger's offices. Epernay seems more connected with the vineyards which are the foundation of Champagne's reputation and beneath its streets and buildings, cut into the chalk, lie over 100 km of cellars where the Champagne is made and matured.

Pol Roger's cellars, holding 7 million bottles, stretch to over 7 km and, at 9˚c, are the coolest in Epernay which, according to Patrice, is one reason for Pol Roger's quality; the second fermentation in bottle is slower at lower temperatures giving a deeper flavour as well as finer bubbles. Patrice is also keen to point out that no wines at Pol Roger see any wood, which means that they remain fresher. This must be a strange departure for the Pol Roger Chef de Cave, Dominique Petit, who was previously Chef de Cave for Krug where wooden barrels are used. To achieve what they see as greater finesse, Pol Roger use only the juice from the best first pressings of the grapes and reject the 'taille' used in lesser Champagnes.

Of over 300 million bottles of Champagne sold every year, 180 million are sold in France, 40 million in the UK and 20 million in the USA. For the better brands, the UK is the most important market because a huge part of the French sales is cheap 'buyers own brand' Champagne. Pol Roger has another major connection with England - it was Sir Winston Churchill's Champagne of choice and indeed they have named their prestige cuvée after the great man.

Our tasting was conducted in a bright room lit by natural sunlight with a splendid marble tasting table with inbuilt spittoons and stools of just the right height on which to perch easily while tasting.

First up was the Pol Roger Brut Reserve White Foil, their standard non vintage. With its delightful fresh nose, it is an excellent crisp, dry, elegant and fruity wine and one which I enjoy on many occasions as an aperitif. However, despite its 33% Pinot Noir content, it did not have the body to accompany a cheese with as much flavour as Jean Poccard's 2004 Beaufort d'Alpage. The Beaufort was superb. I had had it specially sent up from La Cremerie du Lac in Annecy. It was full of flavour and quite wonderful.

Although the Cuvée Sir Winston Churchill 1996 is predominantly Pinot Noir, creating a Champagne in the style of 50 years ago, and a stunning wine in its own right, it somehow didn't seem to suit the Beaufort; it was delightful but seemed a little too soft for the cheese.

It was Pol Roger 1998 Vintage which provided a near perfect match for the cheese. With its 60% Pinot Noir content and 40% Chardonnay, it was robust but refreshing and had all the body that was needed. It had a beautiful pale gold colour, with delightful, fruity, nutty aromas and was far more complex in flavour, with far greater depth and elegance than the Brut Reserve. It combined with the Beaufort to create a delightful spiciness and the combination really brought out the best in both the wine and the cheese.

As is appropriate, this tasting served as an appetiser for a thoroughly enjoyable lunch at Les Berceaux, where I had been all those years ago. Recently modernised, the food seemed to be even better now.

## ❖ Cheese Families

I like to think of cheese in family groups. Within the family the cheeses will share some common characteristics but each member of the family will have its own unique character; where the families come from, the ingredients which make up the family (i.e. is the milk cows', sheep's or goats') and the way the cheeses are made will all help define the character of any individual cheese but, in choosing a cheese, the first consideration must be the family it comes from. Here are my families:

*The Hards* are a dense family. They depend for their appeal on a certain brut-force and strength of character but the best of the family have learned to combine this strength with a certain finesse and complexity. With names like Montgomery Cheddar and Daylesford they have intellect as well as brawn and they are the true stars of this family. Their sheep and goat cousins are a delight, while those from the mountains have a very special appeal.

*The Crumblies* have three main members, Cheshire, Lancashire and Caerphilly. They are notorious for a tendency to crumble if handled roughly but they have an endearingly delicate yet complex flavour.

*The Blues* are best thought of as two rugby teams. The British Blues, such as Stilton, are full-bodied and powerful with massive physiques. Their combined pack weight easily surpasses the French Blues. The French, however, have finesse and subtlety in their favour. Fourme d'Ambert and his siblings are fleet of foot, lighter and more agile.

*The Softies* are at their best when creamy and yielding, but that does not imply that they are without substance. The best amongst them can be either strong or delicate but always complex. Brie and Camembert are the most famous members of this family, but don't forget the goat contingent and youngsters like Mozzarella.

*The Pungent* family are closely related to the softies but are set apart by their strong smell, which is attributable to a bath they have in a liquid such as brine, wine or brandy. Often from northern or eastern France they have names like Pont L'Evêque and Munster.

PARTNERS ON THE TABLES OF LYON

## ❖ St Marcellin: Etoile du Vercors

For pure enjoyment, St Marcellin has few rivals. It is an uncomplicated cheese: soft, smooth, rich and creamy, made from cows' milk and to be eaten within a few weeks of making.

Although it has been made in the stunningly beautiful Isère region, bordering the Alps, since the 15th century, St Marcellin can attribute much of its fame to its presence, since the 1960's, on the cheeseboards of so many of the great restaurants of Lyon.

The original 15th century cheeses were quite hard because, being so small, they dried out easily. They were made from goats' milk until the early 18th century, when there was a re-planting of forests for timber which led to a reduction in the number of goats grazing the hill-sides. Cheesemakers made up the shortfall with cows' milk.

It was not until the 1960's when the cheesemaker, Jean Berruyer, was looking for new markets in Lyon, that a softer cheese was developed – still to this day called 'à la Lyonnaise'. It was then that St Marcellin's fame was assured. Jean had created a winner. The soft, cows' milk cheese proved immensely popular and now dominates the market, although a few, more mature, harder cheeses are still sold in the locality.

Jean started his business in 1942 and called it Etoile du Vercors - Star of Vercors - after the dramatic, mountainous Parc de Vercors, at the foot of which lies the town of St Marcellin, some 50 km west of Grenoble. At the time, the area was a centre for the Resistance and the rugged mountains and valleys must have provided ideal places for the maquis to seek refuge. Jean must have been quite a character because he developed his business into the leading maker of St Marcellin. Today over 100 farms are needed to supply their milk –

50,000 litres every day. Inside their dairy they employ 180 people to make the cheese.

But, just because the business is big, it doesn't mean that they have forsaken traditional methods. On the contrary, it is because they insist on maintaining traditional methods to ensure the quality of their cheeses that they need to employ 180 people. Small basins holding just 75 litres, enough to make 90 small cheeses, are still used to form the curd, which is left in the basins from one day to the next to slowly develop. The next morning 60 people carefully ladle the curds into moulds using small scoops. That this is carried out by hand is a vital part of the process, for no machine has yet been designed which can treat the curds as gently as the human touch. The cheeses are left in their moulds for 2½ hours and then turned, sprinkled lightly with salt, and left for 24 hours. They are now ready to come out of the moulds and pass into the first of the affinage rooms. Over some 3 weeks, they are allowed to lose part of their moisture, initially by natural drying in a warm breeze of some 20˚c, and finally to develop their delightful, soft, creamy texture, at a cooler 10˚c. At any one time, there can be a million of these tiny cheeses waiting to be enjoyed.

Pierre Jacquet, the director of the dairy, enjoys a red or white wine from the Crozes Hermitage or St Joseph vineyards some 30 miles west, when he eats St Marcellin. But I like a young, fruity Beaujolais with this delicate cheese. The texture is creamy and supple to the feel, the aroma is milky and, although quite mild in flavour, it is incredibly rich, with a hint of the lactic acidity of soured milk, not unlike clotted cream. I find it particularly attractive at about 6 weeks of age when a blue/grey mould is just starting to grow.

### ❖ Other light creamy cheeses

St Félicien is almost identical to St Marcellin; being made in the same way in the same area, but nearly twice the size and with a higher fat content.

Chaource is less creamy and more salty and a little more dense than St Marcellin, but is still quite a lot lighter in texture than other soft cheeses such as Camembert.

Brillât Savarin, named after the renowned chef, has a great richness of flavour. Sometimes the cheese is disappointing and the best maker I have found is Delin.

Finn is a sort of English version of Brillât Savarin, made by Charlie Westhead in Herefordshire.

## ❖ Beaujolais Cru Juliénas 2003: Domaine Matray

Lyon promoted to fame not only St Marcellin cheese but also the wines of Beaujolais. In many of the restaurants and bistros of Lyon, St Marcellin and Beaujolais are pretty well the quintessential cheese and wine pairing. The uncomplicated pleasure of a young fruity Beaujolais and a creamy St Marcellin is one of life's more easily accepted experiences. Lyon, that great gastronomic city sitting at the confluence of the rivers Rhône and Soane, is often said to have a third river flowing through it, the Beaujolais! The wines of the Beaujolais have often been thought of as light, frivolous, quaffing wines and indeed some of them are just that. This image was boosted, to the point of excess, over many years when the annual race to get Beaujolais Nouveau to the wine bars of Paris and London distracted attention from the quality of the wine. It also drove down prices as merchant vied with merchant to offer not only the first Beaujolais but also the cheapest.

But putting all that to one side, we are left with a number of producers who make lovely wines. Many of the best are from the ten villages or 'cru' of Beaujolais: Fleurie, Morgon, Juliénas, Moulin à Vent, Brouilly, Côte de Brouilly, St Amour, Régnié, Chiroubles and Chénas. The wines vary from village to village and producer to producer. Some are more full-bodied, some lighter and more fruity. Some age well, others should be drunk young. The lightest wines are overpowered by St Marcellin. The most robust wines, like Chénas, can lack the delightful happy fruit so typical of the Beaujolais region. For matching with St Marcellin, one of my favourites is Juliénas, which often seems to me to have just the right balance between youthful fruit and a structure to partner cheese. I recently tried Juliénas Les Paquelets 2003 from Domaine Matray and it proved just right with the St Marcellin from Etoile de Vercors.

At their vineyard in the delightful village of Juliénas, Lilian Matray and his wife, Sandrine, represent the fifth generation to work the estate. They have just over six hectares in Juliénas plus five hectares in the Saint Amour and Beaujolais Villages appellations. Here they tend the Gamay vines which give the typically fruity and easy-drinking style of wine for which Beaujolais is world famous. It is thought that vines have been cultivated here since the time of Julius Caesar, after whom, perhaps, the vineyard is named. With a south, south-east aspect, Lilian Martray's vines are perfectly placed to ripen beautifully. He generally harvests in mid September but 2003 was the earliest harvest for over 100 years. Lilian insists that all the grapes are picked by hand so as to be better able to sort the grapes and discard any poor ones; something not achieved with a picking machine.

Lilian says of his approach to wine making: "Wine is first and foremost a 'terroir' (that alchemy of land, microclimate, grape variety and not least the vine grower himself). It is also a profession and, above all, a passion. Sandrine and I look after all the work in the vines from pruning to harvest, which remains manual. Following on from this is the winemaking itself, right up to sales. Each stage is inseparable and receives as much care and thought as the last."

Lilian and Sandrine's Juliénas has aromas of violet, raspberry and blackcurrant. Relatively deeply ruby coloured for a Gamay, it is nonetheless quite light in comparison to most red wines. On the palate it is vigorous and brimming with rich fruit flavours of cherry, strawberry, raspberry and blackcurrant.

## ❖ Cuisine à la Lyonnaise

Just south of Lyon, the river valley narrows, and the wide plain and gently rolling hills of Beaujolais are replaced by steep-sided slopes, on which the vines hang precariously.

At Condrieu, where the river bends gently to the east, sits Hôtellerie Beau Rivage. The building itself is of no great architectural merit but the welcome is warm and the impression one of quality. Already there is an air of the South of France. At the tables under the chestnut trees, diners on their way south can look forward to lazy days under a Provençal sun; for those on their way north, it is perhaps a last reminder of all they have enjoyed before returning to the bustle of Paris or cooler climes further north.

It seems a million miles from Lyon, but in fact is only 30 kms and chef Reynald Donet's menu is very much in the style of Lyon which, of course, means that St Marcellin and Beaujolais are served alongside the more local wines and cheeses.

One speciality I enjoyed was a mulled wine sorbet. Simply delicious.

## ❖ Keeping cheese at home

Cheeses are intended to mature as a whole cheese, not as slices; so you should not keep cut cheeses for too long; a few days is generally the longest you should keep a slice. Buy 'little and often' should be your motto and eat the cheese as soon as possible after you have bought it.

Having said that, inevitably, you are going to need to store cheese from time to time. If this will be for more than a few days, try to buy a whole cheese; a small one maybe. A whole Camembert, which weighs 250g, will keep better than a 250g slice of Brie de Meaux. It is more difficult to do this with hard cheeses because, to get the best quality, hard cheeses generally need to be made in large sizes. A small cheddar of less than, say, 5 kg is never as good as a cheddar made in the traditional 25 kg size. So all I can recommend here is to buy the largest wedge you possibly can, as this will keep better than a small slice. Such a wedge of cheese should keep reasonably well for a week to ten days.

Even keeping cheese for a few days requires you to follow certain principles, although how these are interpreted will vary from cheese to cheese and even from season to season. In general cheeses kept at higher temperatures will mature more quickly whereas lower temperatures will retard maturation.

I am often asked "Should I keep my cheese in the refrigerator?" The ideal answer is "No" because most fridges are set at about 4°c which is too cold for most cheeses. Do you have somewhere which is naturally cool? A cellar is ideal; or a garage or an unheated room. Although professional affineurs will mature different cheeses at different temperatures, for the purposes of relatively short-term storage at home, 10°c is a pretty good temperature to aim for and suits most cheeses. True aficionados amongst you will follow my example and have a separate cheese fridge set at 10°c. It works a treat. If you use your regular fridge, just make sure the cheese is well wrapped and keep it for as short a time as possible. Too cold a temperature and the cheese will crack and dry out; too hot and it will ooze an oily fat and become mushy. I do not recommend freezing cheeses as it is likely to affect the texture or consistency of the cheese. Hard cheeses tend to crumble, while soft cheeses lose their delicacy of texture. Flavours are not generally affected too much by freezing.

The other important point when storing cheese is humidity. Generally there is more risk of low humidity leading to hard cheeses which crack and soft cheeses which dry out; but occasionally too high a humidity may result in the excessive growth of moulds on the cheese. For the scientific amongst you, a relative humidity of 80 – 90% is ideal. A low temperature makes it much harder to achieve a high humidity.

Keeping the cheeses covered is likely to be the most practical way to maintain their humidity. Over many years I have tried a number of different wrappings for cheese and I find that the best is waxed paper. Do not use wrappings such as cling film, or other plastic wrappings, which do not allow any moisture to escape from the cheese, leading to soggy cheeses which quickly acquire off flavours. Waxed paper allows the cheese to breath whilst protecting it sufficiently to stop it drying out. I use kitchen foil for many blue cheeses because it maintains more moisture than waxed paper and, I find, blue cheeses aren't generally so susceptible to becoming soggy. Keep cheeses like Camembert, which come in their own little boxes, in those boxes. Keeping cheese in a closed container such as a sealed plastic box may encourage mould growth but do not be afraid of moulds, they are an integral part of many cheeses (for example the white mould on Brie and the blue mould in Stilton). But if you find them unattractive, you can always scrape them off – the cheese underneath will be fine.

'Best Before' dates and 'Use By dates' need a little explanation. Cheeses are notorious for ripening at unpredictable rates, and it is therefore extremely difficult to set a date by which they should be eaten. The best one can hope for is that the cheesemaker, using his experience, can give his opinion of the date by which the cheese is likely to be at its peak. That is why most cheeses carry a 'Best Before' date. It does not mean that the cheese will definitely remain good until that date, nor that it will be bad as soon as the date has passed.

Your cheesemonger should advise you on the maturity of a cheese and, if they advise that the cheese is still in good condition, don't let the date worry you. I have had cheeses which are better after their date than before and I have had cheeses which I would not eat, even before their date.

Use By dates are not, in my view, appropriate for ripened cheeses because it is actually illegal to sell a product which has passed its 'Use By' date.

## ❖ Today's Food

Despite the gastronomic delights of Hôtellerie Beau Rivage and many equally good restaurants in the UK, there is currently a widespread questioning of the direction in which our food production and distribution is heading, especially in retail shops. Coming out at the far side of this debate is a realisation that we have taken some wrong decisions regarding the mass production and over-processing of our food. High salt, sugar and fat levels, which the government is now trying to highlight through a 'traffic light' scheme, are the standard bearers of what I hope will be a move towards 'New Agriculture'. In the words of Slow Food, 'New Agriculture' is "a productive philosophy that is based on quality, biodiversity, respect for the environment, animal well-being, landscape and the health and the enjoyment of the consumer. This agriculture is part ecological and part gastronomic, and it throws aside the outdated and self-destructive parameters of quality (with instant, high profits and high long term costs). With this 'New Agriculture', we also throw aside dioxides, mad cow disease, overdosed anti-parasite treatments and chemical fertilizers, intensive breeding, added colouring, preservatives, flavour additives and all the rest."

The seemingly endless quest to eat more cheaply is flawed because, although the price of food may come down, we pay for it in other ways, as many costs of apparently cheap food are hidden; such as transport costs subsidised by the tax payer through the provision of roads; obesity costs subsidised through the National Health Service; farming subsidies financed through the EU's Common

Agricultural Policy.

So, if you would like greater diversity in your food, more naturally produced foods, healthier foods and a more pleasant shopping experience, here are some suggestions as to what you can do about it. They're not gospel but may help you to enjoy your food just that little bit more:

- ✓ PAY A LITTLE EXTRA. Reallocate your spending budget with a little more on food and a little less on other things. Treat yourself to good food.

- ✓ COOK MORE YOURSELF. Buy less pre-prepared food. Use fresh ingredients.

- ✓ BUY FROM INDEPENDENT SPECIALIST SHOPS, farm shops, organic box schemes etc. Small producers depend on independent retailers for their market. So, if the retailers go out of business, so do the producers and we end up with our food being mass-produced and over-processed, because that is what the big producers and retailers do best. Specialist producers are often too small to supply even one branch of a supermarket and in any case the difference in business culture between the two is often so great that they are unable to do business together. Over 75% of food is now sold through just 4 chains of supermarket (Tesco, Sainsbury, Asda & Morrisons). Include all multiples and the figure rises to a staggering 88%. Be individual and buy small.

- ✓ BUY LOCALLY PRODUCED FOODS. Buy imported foods only if they cannot be produced in this country.

✓ WRITE TO YOUR LOCAL COUNCILLOR, MP & MEP
  - o Ask why regulations are strangling artisan food businesses
  - o Ask why government policy encourages food imports and does not support farmers and the rural community
  - o Suggest schools bring back home economics
  - o Request they ensure that regulations are appropriate to each business they control
  - o Ask them to ensure that legislation and enforcement are proportionate to the risk
  - o Ask them to provide compensation to businesses affected by circumstances beyond their control (eg TB in herd)
  - o Ask the Monopolies Commission to limit any one supermarket to 10% of the UK food market
  - o Ask local planners to limit the size of any store to 20,000 sq ft.
  - o Ask local planners to impose restrictions on large stores; such as part of the car park to be available for a weekly farmers market and guaranteeing 15% of produce is produced locally to the store

✓ TREAT FOOD AS IMPORTANT. Discussing food is good fun. I love finding out more about the food I eat. Pass on the good news about special foods which you find. Above all, take time over your food. We all live busy lives, but time set aside for meals pays huge dividends in improved lifestyle.

Traditional artisan producers have had a hard time over the last half-century. There are opportunities for them now, but only if you support quality foods by patronising independent shops and buying locally-produced foods. Many specialist food shops find their sales increase hugely at Christmas; but why not use them all year round? They won't survive if they're not busy throughout the year. Good food is not just for Christmas.

FRANCE LOSES A WAR: THE WORLD GAINS A CHEESE

## ❖ Brie de Meaux: Fromagerie Dongé

The authorised Brie de Meaux production area covers a large area of gently rolling but predominantly flat countryside, stretching east, roughly between the rivers Seine and Marne, from the eastern suburbs of Paris, through the Ile de France and Champagne provinces, to the borders of Lorraine. Fromagerie Dongé, way out at the eastern extremities of the Champagne region in the small village of Triconville, is a family affair. It was established by Etienne Dongé in the 1930's and is now run by his grand-daughter Madeleine Dongé and her two sons; Luc Dongé is the salesman and Jean-Michel Dongé the cheesemaker. Now employing 45 people, they are one of the finest makers of that legendary cheese, Brie de Meaux. I say legendary because, along with Camembert, it is perhaps France's best known cheese. The two cheeses are, in fact, very similar – apart from their size. Brie de Meaux weighs in at just under 3 kg and is some 35 cm in diameter. Camembert weighs only 250g with a diameter of 11 cm.

Brie has been made in the region certainly since AD 774, when Charlemagne is said to have approved of it, and probably for long before that. But it was in the early 19th century when the cheese came to the attention of the world. As the Congress of Vienna dragged on from 1814 to 1815, the diplomats who had assembled to decide how to organise the states of Europe in the aftermath of Napoleon's defeat, chose to discuss the merits of each nation's cheeses at one of their many banquets. Talleyrand, the great French diplomat, brought a wheel of Brie de Meaux and, no doubt after much discussion, this was acclaimed by those present to be 'Le Roi des Fromages.' Prince Metternich is quoted as saying that although France may have lost a war, the world had gained a cheese! And the world took Brie to its heart, not only making it perhaps the most easily recognised of cheeses but also making copies in their own countries.

At that time, the region was dominated by dairy herds grazing extensive pastures. But, from the last half of the 19th century, the region has been beset by wars which have left their mark. The Franco-Prussian War, The First and Second World Wars were all fought over this countryside causing massive destruction. The number of dairy cows, farms and dairies was dramatically reduced and when cheesemaking was gradually re-established in the 1950's and 60's it was generally of an industrial nature.

When I visited Fromagerie Dongé, Jean-Michel showed me round with evident pride. The ripened evening milk is mixed with morning milk and poured into large basins. It takes 25 litres of milk for every cheese and the appellation contrôlée rules specify that this must be unpasteurised. Jean-Luc adds animal rennet and a natural live starter culture. The curd is cut with a knife resembling a sword and then transferred, using hand ladles, into tallish moulds, with secondary, shorter moulds outside. As the whey drains and the curds subside, the tall moulds are removed and the shorter ones are tightened. When Jean-Luc considers the time is right, the cheeses are taken out of the moulds and sprinkled with salt and sprayed with the penicillium mould spores which will grow into the white fluffy coating on the rind of the cheese. At no point is the cheese pressed; just drained naturally, which means a lot more moisture is retained.

For about seven weeks the cheeses are carefully ripened under Jean-Michel's critical eye before they are ready for dispatch. Jean-Michel considers the ripening to be just as important as the making in achieving a Brie de Meaux of great quality. He is always anxious that his cheeses will be well looked after for the final 1 to 3 weeks after they leave his care and before they are eaten.

The surface penicillium mould on the rind means Brie de Meaux, like all soft bloomy-rind cheeses, ripens from the outside towards the centre. That is why an under-ripe Brie de Meaux will have a chalky layer in the middle. You can tell if a Brie de Meaux is ready to eat firstly by looking at it. The rind should be velvety with slight reddish brown flecks. If the rind is totally white it is probably an industrial cheese and likely to be bland. If the pigmentation is too much, with heavy brown patches, especially around the edge, the cheese is likely to be too old and will taste sharp and aggressive. Secondly, smell it. It should smell fruity. If there is no smell, it is likely to be too young or industrial. If you smell ammonia it is likely to be over ripe. Thirdly feel it. It should be gently yielding from the outer edges to the centre. If the edges yield but the centre is hard, it indicates that the centre will still be chalky and it is not yet ready. If it is very soft everywhere, it is likely to be too ripe. Soft cheeses should be supple and yielding in texture, never runny. You need to chose your Brie carefully because, once cut, the cheese will no longer continue to ripen properly.

Brie de Meaux can be a temperamental cheese, ripening well or badly for seemingly unfathomable reasons. Occasionally, one comes across a 'dead' Brie, which refuses to ripen and stays stubbornly solid. At other times, the cheese can become runny almost over night. The summer can be a particularly difficult time, even with today's refrigeration. Of all the different makers I find Dongé to consistently offer the best cheeses. The cheese I tasted recently was superb, giving off an enticing faint whiff of mushrooms and with an appearance which was sufficiently rustic to be interesting but not too shabby to cause alarm. Once cut into, the buttery-coloured paste was revealed, gently bulging from between the rind without ever quite loosing its shape. No hint of ammonia. The flavour was full and fruity with hints of mushrooms and even sherry but above all opulent and rich.

### ❖ Other deliciously creamy soft cheeses

Brie de Melun is the other great Brie cheese. Some say it is the original, though this is disputed. Smaller in size and bigger in flavour than Brie de Meaux about sums it up although I would add that, to me, the bigger flavour also means less finesse. Unusually, rennet is not used and coagulation of the curd is effected just by lactic fermentation which takes longer. Melun is a town some 50kms to the south of Meaux and the production area is similar but slightly smaller.

Brie de Coulommiers, or Coulommiers for short, completes the triangle of towns which have given their names to Brie cheeses. It is smaller again than Melun being some 15 cm in diameter. Often the mildest of the three, its small size makes it the most convenient to buy as it will keep well until required for eating.

Camembert is another French cheese of global fame but, once again, there are far more poor examples than great ones. The first thing is to look for 'Camembert de Normandie', 'Au Lait Cru' and 'Moulé à la Louche' on the label. With those three, the chances are that the cheese should be good. A particular favourite of mine is made by Reaux at Lessay on the Cherbourg peninsular. It is quite a big dairy, turning out 3 million Camemberts a year, but they achieve a great quality by replicating exactly what would be done on a small scale. So the vats are small and they employ 10 times as many people as a dairy producing one tenth of their output; they don't cut corners to achieve economies of scale, as would all too often be the case in England.

I recently tasted a great new cheese, St Eadburgha, from a farm on the edge of the Cotswolds. It's soft, creamy, gooey and full-flavoured with hints of mushrooms and bitter chocolate. It goes really well with Bourgogne Rouge 2001 from Jean Raphet. Michael Stacey has an organic dairy farm at Willersey, just outside the pretty, tourist village of Broadway. With the plummeting milk price – I know its not plummeting in the supermarkets but the price to farmers is now virtually less than the cost of production – he has decided to do something about it. He has always made a bit of cheese for himself and now he makes it for others. He goes to three farmers' markets where he sells all he produces, and is now installing a bigger vat and a new cheese room. It will still be quite small but big enough to supply some shops too.

Michael also makes St Kenelm which has a harder texture with an interesting and complex flavour yet quite mild — reminds me of fresh flowers. I think it is even better that St Eadburgha.

Waterloo is a stunning cheese from Anne Wigmore; full of flavour, as soft as Brie or Camembert but far sturdier in character.

## ❖ Chinon Les Varennes du Grand Clos 2003: Domaine Joguet

The red wines of the Loire can be tricky to produce and variable in quality. The Loire is, after all, one of the most northerly areas where grapes can be expected to ripen regularly. I find that Chinon, with its impressive Château overlooking the River Vienne near its confluence with the Loire, consistently offers the best red wines from the Loire.

The Château was originally three separate castles and was fortified as long ago as the 12th century by the Counts of Anjou and the Kings of England. It is famous as being the place where Henry II of England died in 1189, and where Joan of Arc met Charles VII of France in 1429. Today it is easy to imagine oneself back in those times as the cobbled streets of the old town are without cars and are lined with ancient houses of wood, brick and stone.

The vineyards which surround Chinon have been planted since time immemorial and are on two major soil types: sandy gravel producing light, fruity wines for early drinking; and limestone which produces wines of greater structure which can age beautifully. In all some 1,900 hectares on which the Cabernet Franc grape achieves greatness. It does not like climates which are excessively hot, and the mild climate of the Loire suits it perfectly. Often regarded as the poor relation of the grapes grown in Bordeaux, here it reigns supreme, giving wines with wonderful higher notes of grassy herbaceous fruit balanced by an attractive earthiness which gives them structure and staying power.

Charles Joguet was first and foremost a philosopher, poet and sculptor, for which he trained in Paris, only becoming a vigneron following his father's death in 1957. He and his widowed mother set about doing something with their vineyards. Charles brought his intellect to winemaking. Hitherto, like other vignerons at the time, his father simply sold the wine in bulk, but Charles had the idea of not only selling it in bottle but keeping the wines from each parcel of vines separate so that they would really reflect their terroir. He also decided to keep the wine from vines of different ages separate. Not for Charles the usual practice, at the time, of blending to produce a single cuvée. He was constantly innovating: new plantings, re-plantings, using only cuttings from his own vines when replanting, limiting yields, using stainless steel vats, picking into smaller crates so as not to crush the grapes prematurely. It was to be hard work but ultimately very rewarding, with Charles being recognised as a gifted winemaker and something of a living legend.

In 1997, forty years after taking over the domaine, Charles decided to "pass the torch" to colleagues and friends with whom he was already working and whose "philosophy resonates with my own values and concepts". It was to take three men to fill the gap left by Charles. Ownership of the domaine passed to Jacques Genet with Alain Delaunay looking after the commercial activities and, since 2005, Francois-Xavier Barc responsible for the winemaking. Charles Joguet was a hard act to follow.

Les Varennes du Grand Clos is a 4½ hectare parcel of vines planted between 1962 and 1976. It sits on clay-chalk soil with some silica, at the foot of a gravely terrace on the left bank of the River Vienne in Sazilly, some 8 km to the east of Chinon. The 2003 is still young but partnered Luc Dongé's Brie de Meaux extremely well. The lovely, refined, fruity nose presages a rich, concentrated wine with plenty of blackcurrant and raspberry ripe fruit, but some woody tannins need a little more time to blend with the fruit. Francois-Xavier says that the 2003 harvest began on 18th September, two weeks earlier than usual and the earliest in the history of the domaine, finishing on 3rd October, which is when it normally begins! Practically all the bunches of grapes were fully ripe with high sugar levels.

The wines of Chinon were praised in the 16th century by the writer Rabelais, Chinon's most famous son, who is commemorated on the labels of Domaine Joguet. One wonders, however, whether it would not be more fitting to commemorate another intellectual, Charles Joguet himself.

As an alternative match for Luc's cheese, I have no hesitation in returning to Burgundy, as I find Burgundies, especially the reds but also the whites, offer some of the best matches for many soft cheeses. A Burgundy I would chose for this cheese is the simple Bourgogne En Bully 2004 from Rapet Père et Fils in Pernand-Vergelesses, just north of Beaune. The estate is very old and Vincent Rapet treasures a wine-tasting cup, dating from 1792, which belonged to one of his ancestors. It is fuller than the Chinon and red Burgundies are, in general, perhaps more reliable partners to cheeses such as Brie de Meaux.

## ❖ Appellation Contrôlée
### – Roughly translated it means la crème de la crème

So went the slogan promoting French cheeses. But it is more than a slogan because it has more than a grain of truth in it. By controlling the methods and areas of production, standards and authenticity are maintained. Cheddar is uncontrolled and the result is a huge amount of low-standard cheeses; Stilton has been controlled since 1936 and the result is, by and large, cheeses which are at least acceptable. The French set up their Appellation d'Origine Contrôlée (AOC) system in 1935 and recently, in 1992, the European Union set up their Protected Designation of Origin (PDO) scheme which includes a number of British cheeses. Both schemes protect a variety of foods and drinks and work by specifying the place of origin of a product, which can be right down to individual fields, and methods of production. In the case of cheeses, control factors can include the type and breed of animal, feeding routines - such as feeding hay not silage in winter for instance - whether the milk may be pasteurised and length of affinage.

## ❖ The Pasteurisation Debate

Brie de Meaux is one of many French cheeses where the appellation contrôlée specifies that the cheese must be made from unpasteurised milk. Pasteurisation has both benefits and disadvantages. Its principal purpose is to destroy potentially harmful bacteria, but it has a number of side effects. These include:

i) Standardising the flavour of the milk, reducing seasonal variations
ii) Destroying beneficial as well as harmful bacteria
iii) Inactivating flavour-giving enzymes, resulting in cheeses which lack character
iv) Retarding the action of rennet
v) Damaging proteins, fats and minerals leading to a loss of nutrition and taste
vi) Destroying some vitamins

By good animal husbandry, the use of effective starter cultures, correct drying of the cheese, control of acidity and other factors, it is possible to ensure the hygienic purity of the cheese without resorting to pasteurisation.

Despite a few popular misconceptions, I am not aware of any government advice to avoid eating unpasteurised cheeses. Indeed I believe that the right to make and sell unpasteurised cheeses is enshrined in EU law. The Food Standards Agency web site says: "In order to avoid the risk of listeriosis, pregnant women are advised to avoid eating ripened soft cheeses of the Brie,

Camembert and blue-veined types, whether pasteurised or unpasteurised." It is worth noting that it is the style of cheese they are worried about not whether or not it is pasteurised. Hard cheeses like Cheddar or Parmesan or not covered and, in any case, the advice is for pregnant women only, although I might add other 'at risk' groups, whose natural immunity is compromised. For normal, healthy adults the risks of eating unpasteurised cheeses are minimal; food-related illness statistics, in fact, reveal that there is more chance of becoming ill by eating salads than cheese.

ITALIAN TAPAS

## ❖ Parmigiano Reggiano: Giorgio Cravero and Guido Bianchi

In the plain formed by the River Po, and nestling under the Apennine hills, lie the cities of Parma and Reggio Emilia that have given their names to the unique and wonderful cheese called Parmigiano Reggiano.

A special treat for me is to sit with a hunk — there's no other word for it — of Parmigiano, breaking off little pieces to nibble at, while sipping a glass of chilled Manzanilla or dry Oloroso sherry and gently passing the time with friends. The cheese, which provides me with so much pleasure, is still made in essentially the same way as it has been for at least seven centuries, and probably longer, since Benedictine monks drained the marshland and started grazing cattle.

Unlike other cheeses, where the maker is king, the need to mature Parmigiano, often for many years, means that here the man who finances the maturing is king. Indeed, maturing the cheeses is considered more as a banking operation than a craft. With most cheeses, I can easily take you to my favourite maker; but in Parma and Modena it is necessary to pass through the labyrinthine web of dealers, selectors, maturers and wholesalers which surrounds Parmigiano production with secrecy and obscures the identity of individual makers. This system transfers to the dealers all responsibility for sales and marketing methods and the reputations which go with it. 'Provenance' for Parmigiano refers more to the finance house than the maker.

The farms producing the milk for Parmigiano are small, the average herd size being just 20 cows; not enough to make cheese individually, so cooperative dairies are the norm. Quality obviously varies from dairy to dairy and one relies on a maturer, such as Giorgio Cravero whose family have been doing just this for five generations, to select good quality cheeses. I love the cheeses Giorgio selects. They have the crystalline, grainy, crunchy texture typical of Parmigiano, yet melt on the tongue, and really come into a different league of flavour, which soars with excellent, light, high notes and an underlying power; spicy but not sharp, rich in spite of its low fat content, sweet yet nutty, strong but not overpowering.

The system has worked well but there are signs of change. The number of dairies has dropped from 1,652 in 1970 to some 500 today. As a result, many of these are now larger. With increased size comes the possibility of maturing their own cheeses and creating their own identity. A number of farmers with their own herds, who have traditionally sold their cheeses to maturers, are now beginning to keep some themselves and sell them ready aged, cutting out the middle man and preserving their own identity in their cheeses.

And then there are those like the Bianchi family, who have their own 40 hectare farm, who are members of the local cooperative, where their cheese is made, and who then age their cheeses and sell them themselves. In effect they are using the cooperative as an expert 'contract' maker. Guido Bianchi, the head of the family, lives on the farm at Basilicanova but his son, Michael, now manages the herd and the milking, which takes place twice a day at 3 o'clock both in the morning and afternoon. As with all farms on the River Po plain, his 250 Friesian cows are kept inside all year round because land is so scarce and valuable. But Michael has recently experimented with allowing the cows out to graze before and after calving. He is a caring person, fond of music, and looks forward to the day when all his cows can roam freely. Mind you, the tobacco-scented hay, which Michael feeds to the cows, is superb; made from Graminacee for fibre and Leguminose for protein, it is full of goodness.

At the Santo Stefano dairy, Pietro Lelli, a second-generation master cheesemaker, oversees the cheesemaking. Milk from the Bianchi farm is kept separate so that Guido's cheeses can be identified with a red 'C' at the end of the process. Out of a total of 60 cheeses made each day by Pietro, 7 cheeses are Guido's.

The production starts when the evening milk arrives and is pumped into shallow vats and left overnight for the cream to rise to the top. In the morning the milk is partly skimmed and mixed with full-cream morning milk, fresh from the cows, and a little of yesterday's whey which acidifies the milk. Once in the deep conical shaped vats, which nowadays are partly underground to facilitate the process, the milk is heated to 30°-35°c, rennet is added and, once the curds have formed, stirred vigorously with a giant, long-handled whisk so that the curd is cut into pieces the size of wheat grains and the temperature is, eventually, raised to 55°c (hotter than for most other cheeses).

When Pietro decides it is time, the curd is scooped into a large, square cloth with wooden paddles and removed from the vat. Two cheeses are made from each vat and very heavy work it is for the men involved. Each cheese weighs in excess of 40 kg. Wrapped in its cloth jacket, the new cheese is placed in a wooden or plastic girdle and left to drain for the rest of the day. In the late afternoon the girdle and cloth are removed, to be replaced by a metal mould, inside which is a stencil sheet which imprints, in pin dots all over the rind: the distinctive Parmigiano Reggiano logo, the date of make and the dairy's identification number. The cheeses stay three days in these metal moulds and then up to four weeks in huge metal cages submerged in a heavy brine solution.

They are then ready to be transferred to large maturing rooms where they patiently await inspection by the Consorzio del Formaggio Parmigiano Reggiano. During this period of waiting, they are regularly turned and brushed with dry salt. If they meet the rigorous standards of the Consorzio, they are rewarded by being branded with a hot iron. If they fail the test, they are consigned to those little tubs of grated cheese that are such a blot on Parmigiano's reputation. As Aristide, Guido's third son, explained, this examination is conducted by gently tapping the cheese with a small hammer and listening for its 'song'. A sweet song and the cheese passes with flying colours; a few discordant notes and failure is assured. Eventually they are moved to Guido's headquarters in Parma's famous Via Trento which was the original centre of the Parmigiano trade, to wait still longer, until Guido or his eldest son, Alberto, decide they are ready for sale.

A few numbers:

251,000 cows produce the milk on
4,750 farms which supply the milk to
492 dairies which make
3,136,191 wheels of Parmigiano Reggiano each year using
16 litres of milk for each kilo of cheese or
600 litres for each whole cheese

## ❖ Other really hard nibbling cheeses

Really hard nibbling cheeses are to be savoured in small quantities and it is probably one of these that I would take to my desert island. Certainly Rachel took some Extra Mature Gouda to the rainforest where it lasted 10 days in the heat of the jungle, without refrigeration, until finally consumed.

Grana Padano is nearly identical to Parmigiano Reggiano, except that it is produced in a neighbouring province. It is generally sold a little younger so it is marginally softer, moister and more fruity.

Sbrinz, almost certainly the cheese referred to by Pliny as Caseus Helveticus, is believed to be the original which the Italians copied for Parmigiano Reggiano. Whatever the truth, it is a great cheese, slightly creamier than Parmigiano but otherwise very similar.

Proper old matured Gouda is so totally different to the rubbish that is usually sold as Gouda as to be considered a different cheese altogether. At 2 or 3 years of age, it is hard and crumbly, often crystalline, tangy with a hint of butterscotch.

Mimolette was first produced in the 17th century in north-east France at a time when the import of Dutch cheeses was banned. Hence it is similar in nearly all respects to aged Gouda except that it is a deep russet colour, is spherical in shape and is attacked by cheese mites as part of the maturing process, leaving it pitted and looking somewhat like a rusty old cannonball.

Coolea is a cheese made in south-west Ireland in the style of Gouda by a Dutchman called Dick Willems and it is exceptionally good.

Pecorino is the Italian word for sheep and is used to describe any cheese made from sheep's milk; so the variety of styles, textures and qualities is extremely wide. Many come from Sardinia and are very good. In Rome they serve the local variety, Romano. But I like best the aged cheeses made in Tuscany, with their intense, savoury, herby, peppery flavours.

Tête de Moine is a Swiss speciality. To eat it you need a machine called a 'Girolle' which will shave wafer-thin slices of cheese into delicate rosettes. These make unusual and visually interesting aperitifs, with an intense, fruity flavour. Literally translated as Monk's Head, the cheese takes its name from its appearance similar to the shaved patch on the crown of the monks' heads at the Abbey de Bellelay where it is made.

Perhaps the most unusual cheese I have ever tasted is Yak's milk cheese. One day a British cheesemaker, who had visited China, arrived with a small container, no bigger than a cigarette packet; inside were what looked like bent matchsticks. These turned out to be dried curd. This cheese (!) was made in Mongolia where he had been invited to advise the locals on cheesemaking. It was the dairy equivalent of Beef Jerky or Biltong. Very dry, very chewy, quite salty, not a huge amount of flavour; but vaguely dairyish. An experience but not a sure-fire winner on the cheeseboard, I fear.

## ❖ Dry Oloroso Sherry Pata de Gallina: Juan Garcia Jarana

The Italians will drink Lambrusco with Parmigiano but I have never found a Lambrusco which I liked; I prefer Champagne, or better still, one of the diverse styles of sherry. My favourite is a Dry Oloroso. Sipping Dry Oloroso and nibbling Parmigiano in front of a log fire on Christmas morning (or any other morning!) gives a great sense of all being well with the world. A better mid-morning snack is hard to find.

In some ways, sherry is a victim of its own success. Popular in England since Tudor times, its immense popularity, especially in the 1950's and 60's, led in the 1970's and 80's to a degrading of styles and quality. Many of the glorious wines that this corner of south-west Spain can produce were sweetened for export and blended into a pale reflection of their true style. The availability of export subsidies resulted in some dubious transactions whose primary aim was to obtain the subsidy, whilst shipping wine of the lowest quality. Unfortunately this wine eventually found its way on to the market, driving down prices and quality. The large bodegas responded by reducing the quality of all but their premium wines. Fortunately most have seen the error of their ways and the quality of most sherries has now been restored to its rightful level.

Foremost amongst the quality bodegas is Emilio Lustau which, apart from supplying all the usual sherry blends, also offers a range of wonderful 'almacenista' sherries. These come exclusively from some 50 small bodegas and represent sherry in its most pure and classical form, being full of character and individuality. Whilst some may own their own vines, the more usual system is for the almacenista to buy from farmers and introduce their wines into their own solera system for maturing. In the solera system, which is at the heart of sherry production, rows of barrels are stacked in layers. When there is a need for bottling, part of each barrel in the bottom layer, which contains the oldest wine, is drawn off for bottling. The barrels are then topped up with younger wine from the layer above, which refreshes the older wine and, at the same time, takes on some of the character of the older wine. These barrels in turn are topped up from the layer above and so on up the layers to the top of the stack, where the barrels are replenished with the latest harvest. Some of these soleras were laid down as much as 150 years ago. The regulations stipulate that this ageing must be for at least three years but many are aged for much longer.

The Palomino grape, grown on white compact chalky 'albariza' soil, dominates sherry production, although small quantities of Pedro Ximenez often grown on sandy 'arena' or clayey 'barro', land also feature, often for sweetening purposes.

Although sherry is marketed in a sometimes bewildering range of styles, there are in fact only two basic types: Fino and Oloroso. Finos are lighter and more delicate, Olorosos are richer and heavier. But the big difference is that a natural yeast, known as flor, grows on the Finos but not on the Olorosos. The flor prevents Finos from oxidising and gives them their individual character. By contrast the Olorosos depend on oxidation for their character. Much Oloroso is used in the blends for sweet cream sherries.

Dry Oloroso is very much at the specialist end of the spectrum, with patchy distribution and minimal sales. My favourite Dry Oloroso is Pata de Gallina from the bodega owned by Juan Garcia Jarana. Juan's bodega, in the old Santiago quarter of Jerez de la Frontera, is one of the smaller ones; delightful in every way. Like many almacenistas, his main business is not sherry; in his case it is motorcycles. But in 1979 he decided to buy the bodega, which was originally founded in the 19th century, in order to indulge his love of fine sherry.

The Pata de Gallina solera consists of 38 butts (the special sherry barrel containing 490 litres) and the wines are aged for 20 years. Importantly, this Oloroso is dry, as it should be, rather than being sweetened which happens all too often for export. It is a rich russet brown mahogany in colour with a marvellous spicy aroma of dried fruits with hints of leather, oranges and nuts. The delicious lingering flavour has a ripe-fruit sweetness but is classically dry with a raisiny, burnt-caramel flavour reminiscent of prunes and walnuts. This is sherry of the highest quality.

❖ Cooking with cheese

I find that I eat so much cheese in its natural state that I tend to avoid dishes that contain cheese as an ingredient. This is a pity as I miss out on some truly wonderful recipes. Cheese is extremely versatile as an ingredient and can be melted, sliced or grated into many superb dishes, from starters to light simple snacks, to main courses and desserts.

Many people think of 'mousetrap' when choosing cheese with which to cook; this again is a mistake. The French make extensive use of Roquefort and Comté, two of the most expensive cheeses, in their recipes. They do so because, by using a good quality, strong-flavoured cheese they actually need less of it. This means that it is not actually as expensive as it might seem. Needing to use less cheese is also a point worth remembering when it comes to making light dishes such as soufflé, or when counting the calories.

Cheeses that I consider are specifically designed as 'ingredient' cheeses include: Feta, the sharp, salty, crumbly essential ingredient for Greek salads. It should be made from sheep's milk but often is cows' milk or occasionally goats' milk.

Mozzarella should be an essential ingredient for pizzas but all too often is replaced by cheaper alternatives. Genuine mozzarella is made from buffalo milk, is pearl white and has a delightfully mild, lactic, slightly sour flavour. It is delightful sliced and served with tomatoes, olives, basil leaves and anchovies, and seasoned with a little olive oil, salt and freshly ground black pepper.

The classic way to enjoy Raclette is melted and served with new potatoes. Simple, easy and guaranteed to bring back memories of skiing trips.

A WINTER'S TALE

## ❖ Le Mont d'Or (Or Vacherin du Hauts Doubs): Sancey Richard

There is no surer sign that autumn has arrived than the appearance in the shops of Le Mont d'Or. Just as bonfire night, the clocks going back and the first home rugby games signify the end of summer, so Mont d'Or, to me, heralds the imminent change to the gastronomic joys of winter which lie ahead. Made by dairies which make Comté in summer, Mont d'Or remains a seasonal cheese; available only between September and May. It can actually be made only between 15th August and 15th March but the longer period of availability is to allow for ripening.

Mont d'Or has a stunning appearance, a haunting aroma, a satiny smooth texture and a unique resinous flavour, all of which combine to make it a truly remarkable cheese.

It comes wrapped in a circle of spruce bark, to hold it together, and is presented in a wooden box. The spruce bark gives it a vaguely resinous flavour but there are also hints of nutmeg, mushrooms, cabbage and bacon. These are not always strong flavours but they combine together to great effect, and the result is a full and substantial flavour.

The silky smooth texture of the ivory-coloured paste should be softly flowing but can become exceeding runny. Often the best way to serve the cheese is with a spoon!

The cheese takes its name from the Mont d'Or peak in the mountainous Jura region of eastern France, close by the Swiss border. The area is heavily forested, with lots of timber yards and any number of huge lorries carrying felled trees. Interspersed amongst the trees are open pastures, rich in wild grasses in summer, providing ideal grazing for the local Montbéliarde cows which give wonderful milk for making Comté cheese. In winter, however, the region is snow-covered and, while skiers appear as if out of nowhere, the cows are confined to their sheds. They are fed hay made the previous summer (no silage is permitted) which gives milk which is less fruity and paler in colour and often of insufficient quantity to make a whole 30 kg wheel of Comté. So the dairies had the idea of making a smaller, soft cheese instead, and Mont d'Or was born. How blessed we are that they did so, as otherwise we might never have tasted this outstanding cheese.

For over 200 years farmers on both sides of the border have produced the same style of cheese, known as Vacherin de Mont d'Or ; but French production had fallen substantially due to difficulty in distributing the fragile cheese, until the 1960's when it began to rise again. This prompted the Swiss into action and, in the 1970's, they were able to appropriate the name for themselves, forcing the French to call their cheeses either Le Mont d'Or or Vacherin du Haut Daubs. The Swiss now use pasteurised milk, and the Mont d'Or peak itself is in France, so I prefer to think of France as the true home to the cheese. There is no longer any farmhouse production but 11 dairies in France make a total of some 3,500 tons — or nearly 7 million of the small cheeses; a huge increase since 1990 when production was about 700 tons.

The Mont d'Or, which I like best, is made by Patrick Richard, in his dairy in the village of Metabief, right at the foot of the Mont d'Or peak. The dairy is run by the Sancey Richard family of three brothers, mother and sister. They buy in all their milk, which I always think is a bit of a shame, but they have a lot to do as they also run three shops where they sell 40% of their production. A nice little closed business: very low food miles.

Patrick explained to me that a secret skill of getting the right consistency in the cheese is to cut the curd in pieces the size of walnuts and to form a thin skin around each piece so as to retain moisture, a process he called 'coiffe'. Otherwise the cheesemaking process is much the same as for any soft cheese.

Once the cheese is made, it has its protective circle of spruce bark placed around it and held in place by a small, splinter like, peg. Then it is ripened for a minimum of three weeks and preferably four weeks. For the first two weeks the cheeses are turned and brushed with salt water virtually every day and kept at 11°c. Then they are put into their wooden boxes, which are deliberately made a little smaller than the diameter of the cheese. In order to fit the cheese in the box the bark has to be cut with a sharp knife and the cheese squeezed into the box. This has the effect of giving the top rind of the cheese its hallmark appearance of a crumpled flannel with its attractive lightly pinky, beige colour. The temperature is then reduced to 3°c until the cheeses are ready for despatch. In general they are ready for eating within a month of leaving the dairy, but this will vary depending on the ripening carried out by the specialist cheesemonger.

Sanchey Richard's Mont d'Or deservedly won a gold medal at the 2006 Concours Général Agricole in Paris.

I have two favourite ways of enjoying Mont d'Or: firstly accompanied simply by fresh French bread and a glass of Château Chalon and served, ideally, as a mid-morning snack. Secondly baked in the oven and perhaps served with new potatoes and seasoned with a little black pepper.

The first is simplicity itself. You can either cut the cheese, as you would a cake; but this is sometimes difficult if the cheese is particularly runny. Better sometimes to cut off and remove the top surface rind of the cheese, and then either use a spoon or treat it as a fondue and dip your bread into the cheese.

To bake in the oven, first open the box and cut a small hole of 3 to 5 cm diameter in the centre of the cheese. Insert one or two cloves of garlic into the rind if you wish. Pour approx 10cl of dry white wine into the hole you made. Season with black pepper. Replace the wooden lid and wrap a piece of aluminium foil around the complete, closed box. Place in a pre-heated oven at 200°c and bake for 25 minutes. Serve with new potatoes and a bottle of Château Chalon.

## ❖ Château Chalon 1999: Domaine Berthet-Bondet

In my experience, few English people know of Château Chalon and, of those that do, there are some who love it and others that find it simply too daunting to contemplate. I'm firmly amongst the former, especially when drinking it with Mont d'Or which, I find, is the perfect partner.

The 12th century village of Château Chalon is impressively built on a rocky outcrop, which stands prominently above the surrounding valley. Clearly built to be easily defended, the village was also home to a Benedictine monastery which was destroyed in the French revolution. As I approached the village, up the winding road from Voiteur, I could see plenty of vineyards encircling the village but only those with a south or south-west aspect are entitled to grow the grapes for this special wine. The other vineyards must produce the humbler Côtes du Jura. It is from the Jura, with its marl and limestone soils, that the generic name Jurassic is derived.

My destination was the 16th century house of Jean and Chantal Berthet-Bondet, set at the edge of the village in a magnificent setting. Jean and Chantal are first generation vignerons. Having met at agricultural college and sharing a liking for Vin Jaune, they decided to follow their dreams and, in 1985, bought the house and 3 hectares of vines and set about bringing life back to the domaine which had been 'dry' for 50 years. Today they have 10 hectares and produce marvellous wines of great character which I saw ageing in over 500 barrels in their impressive cellars.

So, what is the character of this wine which I have described as daunting, but for which I share a liking with Jean and Chantal? Château Chalon may be considered the Premier Cru of Vin Jaune, or 'yellow wine'. On the nose it is immediately Fino sherry and, indeed on the palate it is reminiscent of sherry. But it is somehow older and deeper in flavour than a Fino. Of course the similarity is not coincidental. It is because both Château Chalon and Fino sherry grow flor yeast on the surface of the wine as it lies ageing in oak barrels of 228 litres. In the case of Château Chalon, this ageing is for a minimum of six years during which time it is forbidden to top up the casks, and almost 40% of the wine is lost through evaporation. It is said that it was one of the monks at the Benedictine Monastery in the village who inadvertently discovered Vin Jaune by forgetting to refill a cask of wine. The flor yeast growing on the surface protects the wine from oxidation but it still takes on many of the characteristics of old white wine and the amount of evaporation intensifies the flavours in the wine. Unlike most wine cellars which are damp, it is essential that the cellars where the barrels are stored should be totally dry and well ventilated to allow the yeast to grow.

Its character is further enhanced by ageing in bottle for anything up to 20 years. There are even examples of exceptional years being aged for over a century. The result is a wine of great intensity with a certain sourness offset by a hint of sugar. The 1999 vintage from Berthet-Bondet has a full, rich aroma and flavour with hints of dried fruits, hazelnuts, almonds, mushrooms, truffles, spices and dried herbs; and yet it retains very appealing light, high notes and possesses great elegance and finesse. Château Chalon is made from Savagnin grapes grown in one of France's smallest appellation areas; just 60 ha. If you can not find Château Chalon, there are other vins jaunes from the Jura, notably Arbois, but you must look carefully for the words 'Vin Jaune' on the label as not all Arbois is. Other vins jaunes generally tend to be a little coarser and less refined than Château Chalon. Increasingly Chardonnay is being planted in the

Jura which produces a pleasant enough wine but it is not vin jaune and can be overpowered by Mont d'Or.

Resist the temptation to serve Château Chalon chilled. It is much better served at just below room temperature (15˚c - 17˚c) and cuts through the creaminess of Mont d'Or to great effect. As well as enjoying Château Chalon with Mont d'Or, I find it goes very well with Foie Gras, to make a mushroom cream sauce for chicken, or simply by itself as an aperitif. Jean recommends it with curry, but I haven't tried this.

Befitting the uniqueness of the wine, Château Chalon has a unique bottle, the Clavelin. This is the only bottle authorised by EU regulations to contain 62cl - a reminder that nearly 40% of every litre is lost to the angels through evaporation.

Vin Jaune sometimes has a bad press from commentators unable to appreciate its unique merits but nonetheless Jean told me that total production remains constant, even increasing a little. It may not be a wine for you but I urge you to try it with Mont d'Or as I did on a grey November day in the Cotswolds. The day lightened as I sipped it and the pairing added to my enjoyment of both wine and cheese.

If you find it is not for you, or can not find any, you can always try a glass of Fino sherry or Champagne or a light fruity Gamay or Chardonnay; all of which are extremely enjoyable with Mont d'Or.

## ❖ The Hygiene Police

During my time as Chairman of The Specialist Cheesemakers' Association, much of my time was taken up battling with the authorities on behalf of cheesemakers who were being given a tough time.

During the 1990's there were two major court battles. Firstly Humphrey Errington, who makes Lanark Blue cheese in Scotland, was told by his Environmental Health Officer that his cheese contained Listeria Monocytogenes and that a 40% mortality rate could be expected. Faced with this frightening prospect, he agreed to their request that he withdraw the cheese from sale. However, when no cases of illness came to light, he thought he should be allowed to sell his cheese. The officials did not agree.

At an initial hearing, before magistrates, the cheese was condemned. A subsequent Judicial Review found that Humphrey had been denied natural justice and a court case before Sheriff Allan followed, during which I gave evidence. This lasted from August to October 1995 and, at the end of the case, Sheriff Allan ruled that the cheese did not fail to comply with food safety requirements. He was scathing about the officials, saying that not all strains of Listeria Monocytogenes are pathogenic, that some of the council's witnesses were unreliable, that the tests results used by the council could not be relied upon, and that their behaviour was tantamount to harassment. He went on to say that enforcement actions by officials should be based on risk assessment and that there was no evidence that the council had done this.

The case was brought at huge expense to the ratepayers of Lanark and Humphrey and his family suffered untold stress. However, at least it was a victory for common sense.

But the sense of relief was short-lived, because the authorities were to have another crack at specialist cheeses in 1998 when a boy was found to have an illness, apparently caused by the bacteria E.Coli 0157.

This time the target was Chris Duckett, who makes Wedmore cheese in Somerset, and one of his customers, James Aldridge. Officials linked the boy's illness to Chris Duckett's cheese and the then Minister for Public Health signed the first ever 'Emergency Control Order', the effect of which was to ban the sale of any cheese made by Chris Duckett. As if that was not bad enough, an emergency control order does not allow anyone to challenge whether or not the cheese is, in fact, unfit for consumption.

Yet this was precisely what James and Chris wanted to do, because their microbiological tests showed nothing wrong with the cheese. Officials were unimpressed, saying that just because no contamination had been found, it didn't mean that it wasn't there — just that it hadn't been found.

James Aldridge, who matured Chris's cheeses, had about £40,000 worth of stock and found himself faced with the prospect of destroying it without compensation, which would have bankrupted his business. The only way James could proceed was to apply for a judicial review of the minister's action. This he did and it was found that the minister had exceeded her powers and that less draconian measures would have sufficed.

The Department of Health appealed, signalling to me that they wanted to have the right to condemn out of hand any food they suspected of being unfit, without the need to pay compensation if they were wrong.

To me this was a denial of natural justice. Surely anyone accused of something should have the right to defend themselves and to compensation if the officials are found to be wrong.

The Appeal Court backed the Minister.

The whole episode had exhausted James. He gave up the fight, accepted the Department of Health's offer of an ex-gratia payment, and died on 5th February 2002. Many people believe that he died of a broken heart.

The Emergency Control Order has not been used since, but it remains on the statute book and hangs like a sword of Damocles over all food businesses.

Since the creation of the Food Standards Agency there have been no more court cases involving specialist cheesemakers, and the relationship between officials and cheesemakers has improved, although it sometimes remains an uneasy one.

I find it hard to have confidence in food safety officials when their actions have been so comprehensively called into question by these two court cases. Further scepticism is warranted by an EU committee's disclosure, in 1999, that microbiological criteria relating to cheese were not established on the basis of a formal risk assessment and that many of the criteria did not appear to be meaningful in terms of consumer health protection.

The concept of zero risk and focussing so intently on food safety seems to have taken hold to such an extent that food's nutritional value and gastronomic qualities are often overlooked or ignored. We need to regain a sense of proportion. As The Times reported on 26th April 1999, in one year, 34 people died from food poisoning compared with 83 who died falling out of bed.

A MODERN CHAMPION

## ❖ Berkswell: The Fletchers

Stephen Fletcher has a quiet, deliberate way about him; seemingly a man who likes to try and foresee the outcome before he makes a decision, he claims to have been totally unprepared for the challenges he would face in cheesemaking and certainly he could not have foreseen the success he would have with his 'new' cheese when he started making Berkswell in 1989.

Now deservedly ranked by many as the finest ewes' milk cheese made in England, when I first met Stephen, the cheese was nothing special. On my first visit I was unimpressed by either the cheese or the dairy and left the farm thinking what a nice idea they had, but that there needed to be some big improvements if they were to make a go of it. And improve they did! The cheese is now one of my firm favourites; one I know I will always enjoy and one I am delighted to find on a restaurant cheeseboard.

Stephen describes two defining moments as being the 1992 Specialist Cheesemakers' conference in Harrogate and the encouragement he felt at the praise he received from other cheesemakers and retailers who tasted his cheese for the first time. This, coupled in the previous year, with the thrill of walking into the room after the judging at the Bakewell Show, to see the rosette indicating he had won first prize.

So what makes the cheese so great? Ask Stephen and he'll say he doesn't know. Ask Linda, his cheesemaker, and she'll say she doesn't know. Pressed, Stephen says they must be doing something right but he doesn't know what. Slowly though he lets out that he considers animal husbandry and feed to be important. Without good milk you can't even hope for good cheese. Stephen looks after the sheep and responds to their needs. He says Friesland sheep have a low health threshold, easily picking up pneumonia and mastitis; they are high-maintenance but are phenomenal when it comes to their milking ability and temperament. Although the tensions, which exist in a herd of cows, are almost absent with sheep, they have a habit of taking on the world, and sometimes coming off second best. They complain at the slightest opportunity; they want to be in a different field from the one they're in; they're choosy about what they eat. But at Ram Hall they're lucky in their diet. The farm may be tucked between Birmingham and Coventry but, although this may sound unromantic, the area is surprisingly, charmingly rural and the grassland here, some of which Stephen reckons has been planted for over 200 years, provides ideal grazing for the ewes.

The palatability of the grass changes seasonally, and even daily, so Stephen needs to keep on top of this and ensure his ewes are happy with their food. The ph of the soil must be right; the length of the grass must be right – Stephen says the ideal length is the height it grows overnight. To help, Stephen also feeds the sheep with a special compound to balance out the grazing, and feeds a mix of grass and maize silage from December to mid April. This must be finely chopped so that the sheep can't be selective and only eat the bits they like. He says that it is like looking after 400 fussy, spoilt children!

Milking the sheep is another major operation, taking as much as seven hours a day; but at least they get some respite in October and November when the sheep are dry.

To a farming family like the Fletchers, who have been at Ram Hall since 1886 and who have recently received an 'Excellence in Practical Farming' award, the animal bit might be considered the easy bit. Making cheese requires different skills. Once the decision was made to use their sheep's milk for cheese rather than simply sell it as liquid, Stephen's mother, Sheila, went off to Otley College in Suffolk to learn to make cheese.

Soon after they started, Sheila was joined by Linda Dutch, who now does most of the cheesemaking; and an excellent job she makes of it. Using the milk fresh from the sheep and unpasteurised, undoubtedly contributes to the quality of the cheese but Linda's skill is critical. Linda explained that, surprisingly for a hard cheese, she does not cut the curd finely but simply into squares and then stirs the curds and whey by hand, before scooping the curd into regular plastic kitchen colanders. She pushes the curd into these colanders by hand in order to expel as much whey as possible and then they are left to drain, being turned regularly and dry salted on each side. The cheeses firm up quite a lot during the first seven days and take on the distinctive pattern created by the holes in the colanders. Further maturing takes a minimum of 3 months but the cheese is really at its best after 6 months. Stephen thinks his finest cheeses are made in February, when the sheep are eating the best silage, and in June when the grazing is at its optimum and with the solids in the milk at their peak.

When they first started they were only just had enough sales to justify making cheese 2 or 3 times a week. Despite a number of knock-backs over the years, now they make two vats a day 5 or 6 days a week for much of the season and each vat produces about 25 three-kilo cheeses.

The finished cheese has a very attractive and interesting, rustic, light amber coloured rind. The interior paste is almost translucent ivory. The texture is firm and, with age, slightly crystalline; the flavour is breathtaking: full, rich, nutty, sweet, caramel-like, fruity and savoury all at the same time, with hints of fresh, rich meadow grass and many layers of flavour, all in total harmony, unfolding as one tastes the cheese.

Ram Hall Farm is just outside the village of Berkswell, which takes its name from a Saxon king, Bercul, who was born in the village and baptised at its well, which still exists today. The king would, I feel sure, be delighted that his name lives on not only as a village but in such a special cheese as well. No records exist of when or why the house was built. Although the name of the house is Anglo-

Saxon, indicating its ancient origins, the present house is almost certainly 16th century and has a delightful air of timelessness about it. There is a room on the first floor of the house which used to be a cheese room at some point in the past. Although what type of cheese was made is anyone's guess, I doubt it was up to the standard the Fletchers have attained.

They are great ambassadors for British cheese: Stephen, Tessa, Linda and Sheila, can often be found at events and exhibitions where their cheese never fails to cause excitement and to impress. It is generous of them to give their time promoting British cheeses and they should be a huge motivation to aspiring cheesemakers. Some 15 years after inventing and making their first cheese, they have scaled the pinnacle of quality to produce some of the very best cheeses available; a modern champion.

## ❖ Other stunning sheep's milk cheeses

Apart from Roquefort, Manchego is probably the best-known sheep's milk cheese, but it is often extremely difficult to find a good one. Made on the plateau of La Mancha in central Spain, the cheese is very hard-pressed and then salted in a strong brine solution. The flavour tends to be herby, sometimes with a hint of olives. It is easily recognised by the zig-zag pattern on the rind, left by the rush grass binder.

Ossau Iraty is the exact opposite of Manchego; not very well known but nearly all the examples I have tasted have been good. Made on the French side of the Pyrenees, Ossau Iraty is a hard cheese with a delightful nutty character.

Wigmore is a delightful sheep's milk cheese with something of a melting chocolate texture; soft and voluptuous. When I first visited Anne Wigmore, I felt I had been inside a Tardis! Outside it was just like a wooden shed at the end of the garden; inside it was a state-of-the art dairy — all stainless steel and white, wipe-down surfaces. Anne and her husband, Andy, have developed the recipe for the cheese themselves, so the cheese is unique and one of the stars of modern British cheesemaking.

### ❖ Fonseca 20-Year-Old Tawny Port

Bruce Guimaraens was one of the world's great port makers. Larger than life in both his stature and his wit, he was responsible for all the ports made by one of the greatest port houses, Fonseca, from 1960 until succeeded by his son in 1994. With one man in charge of so many wines, one might expect a certain style to run through them all. Bruce's style was quality, pure and simple, with each wine exhibiting the best characteristics of the particular port style he was making. I will be looking at Vintage Port in the chapter on Stilton; but for a hard sheep's milk cheese like Berkswell, the ideal accompaniment, for me, is an aged tawny port.

Aged Tawny Ports are matured in wooden vats or casks and come with an indication of age - 10, 20, 30 or 40 years old – and are a blend of wines from different years, the average age of which is that stated. The older the age the lighter the wine, but even at 10 years old they are considerably lighter than a vintage port which is matured in bottle. The variation from one harvest to the next, reflected in vintage ports with only certain years being declared, makes for a good story and generates a natural interest. As a result tawny ports have often been considered of less interest. But, in the hands of a master like Bruce Guimaraens, they are impressive wines.

Bruce grew up with port in his veins; in 1822 his great-great grandfather, Manuel Pedro Guimaraens, bought the nascent business of Fonseca & Monteiro which, like most of the great port houses, had carried on a trade in a wide variety of foodstuffs and cloth since its foundation in the late 1700's. Manuel decided to concentrate on port wine and the family has been involved ever since. Four members of the family have made all the vintages of the last century. It would seem more appropriate for the firm to be called Guimaraens but the departing Fonseca, when he sold his shares in 1822, insisted that his name be retained.

The years immediately after the Second World War were difficult for the port trade and so it was that, in 1948, the ownership of Fonseca became consolidated with another highly respected port house, Taylor Fladgate & Yeatman. My first introduction to Fonseca was through the Chairman of both houses, Alistair Robertson, who explained that although both companies are under the same ownership, from the winemaking point of view they are run quite separately, with Fonseca having its own distinct style. This is confirmed every time I taste ports from the two houses.

What seems like many years ago, Bruce showed me round the centre of Fonseca's vineyards, their 44 hectare estate, Quinta do Panascal, just south west of Pinhão on the River Távora, in the heart of the wild and mountainous Douro region of northern Portugal. The Douro valley is where the grapes for all port are grown and the area is heavily terraced to make the vineyards anything near workable. Still, it is amongst the most difficult of all wine growing regions. Here grows a bewildering variety of grapes; nearly 80 varieties are permitted although it is generally recognised that four, Touriga Nacional, Touriga Franca, Tinta Roriz and Tinto Cão, produce the best wines.

In September or October every year the harvest takes place. In order to extract the fruit, colour and tannins essential to the character of port, it is vital to maintain maximum contact between the skins and the juice during pressing and fermentation. Treading the grapes by foot in large open stone troughs, called lagares, is the traditional and still the best way to do this, and is used extensively by Fonseca. However, it is extremely labour-intensive and, over the years, a number of semi-automatic processes have been tried out with varying degrees of success.

The sweetness of port is achieved by adding neutral grape spirit to the partly-fermented grape juice, thus stopping the fermentation and maintaining some of the natural sweetness of the grapes.

The concentration of so many extracts brought about by the pressing method of the grapes, the shock addition of alcohol and the sudden ending of fermentation, produces raw, rough wines, which need time to mature. Some people complain of hangovers from port. By drinking tawnies or vintage ports, which have been aged for at least 10 years, I have seldom experienced the problem. Avoid younger wines, rubies, Late Bottled Vintage and so-called Premium or Vintage Character ports.

All the newly-made ports are kept at the quinta until the following spring when they are graded and moved to the maturing lodges (above ground cellars) in the town of Vila Nova de Gaia, 75 km down river on the coast opposite the port of Oporto, from which the wine derives its name. Fonseca tawnies are aged in their lodges in Gaia on the bend of the river where the relative humidity is slightly higher, helping to preserve the fruity style that Bruce wanted and which is the hallmark of Fonseca.

The aged tawnies are matured in casks of 550 litres (or pipes as they are called in the Douro). The high surface area to volume ratio of these pipes allows a slight oxidisation to take place while the fresh berry flavours give way to more complex, ripe, plumy fruit and a distinctly nutty character, with hints of caramel, cinnamon and butterscotch, and the appearance of the wine takes on its characteristic russet/tawny hue. As the wines ages they lighten in colour until about 25 years of age, after which they start to pick up colour from the wood; an olive green tone that starts to verge on very dark by 100 years.

Being lighter in style, I find tawny ports are in many ways more suited to modern diets than the richer, more full-bodied vintage ports. I love them with all hard cheeses, except the very strongest, which can overpower the delightful delicacy of a fine tawny. With Berkswell, Fonseca 20-Year-Old is sublime. The wonderful aroma is immediately apparent on opening the bottle; the rich amber tawny colour with russet highlights excites the senses. The ripe, plumy flavour allied to a distinctive spiciness creates a truly magical harmony with Berkswell. Both have a nutty sweetness balanced by a savoury spiciness that are so well matched it can be difficult to separate the flavours of the cheese from those of the port.

I find Fonseca 20-Year-Old Tawny a compelling wine, combining a wonderful richness and power with great finesse and elegance. I consider it a supreme example of the style. In Fonseca 20-Year-Old Tawny, Bruce Guimaraens established a character which is, to me, the outstanding example of this style of port. Bruce once said to me that to make a good port one needs good beer. It took me a few seconds to realise that the 'good beer' was intended to be drunk by Bruce, not to go into the blend! I met Bruce in Portugal and in London and it seemed to me the two things he enjoyed most were the company of others and making wine; he excelled at both. Many, as I do, will remember his enthusiastic conversation. Many more will remember his glorious wines.

## ❖ How to Make Cheese

The first thing is to make sure the quality of the milk is really good. Good cheese can not be made without good milk. The breed of animal will have a huge effect on the style of cheese. Not only the breed, but its feed, age and stage of lactation are important in determining the quality of the milk and thus the cheese.

Milk will vary from day to day, depending on what the animals have been eating (wild garlic is a nightmare) and even the weather (thundery weather can produce tough cheeses). One of the biggest differences is between summer cheeses, from cows fed on grass, and winter cheeses, from cows fed on silage. Both have their merits but some French appellation contrôlée regulations specify that hay, not silage, must be fed in winter and some cheesemakers even have grass driers, for years when the sun is not enough. I have tried asking English farmers to consider installing a grass drier, only to be met with a blank stare.

Large industrial cheesemakers standardise the milk from several farms so that they can produce a consistent, if sometimes bland, quality.

The artisan cheesemaker works with milk which is marginally different every day. So what he produces will be more individual in character; varying slightly from day to day which is part of their charm.

Once the milk is in the vat, there are further choices for the cheesemaker. Reduce the fat by skimming the milk, or add extra cream. Mix the morning and evening milk or keep them separate. Perhaps the biggest question is whether to pasteurise or not.

At the heart of the cheesemaking process is the separation of the curds and whey. First a live bacterium, known as a starter culture, is added to sour the milk, converting lactose into lactic acid. The choice of starter culture can have a big effect on the flavours which are in the cheese. Some work quicker than others, some work best at different temperatures, some tolerate salt better than others. Some are freeze dried; others are liquid. With the liquid ones, it is necessary to use a different strain each day of the week and, quite often, I have selected cheeses from several different days, only to find they have all been made using the same starter; one which gives a flavour I find particularly attractive.

The next stage is the addition of rennet to hasten the separation of curds and whey. Rennet is an enzyme from the lining of a calf's stomach. These days a vegetarian substitute is sometimes used, especially in Britain, where it is seen as a marketing point to sell 'vegetarian' cheese. Some rennet substitutes are natural, for instance thistles, but most are genetically modified. They can give a bitter taste to cheeses and many cheese connoisseurs prefer cheeses made with traditional, animal rennet.

The temperature now is absolutely critical. A high temperature will expel whey from the curd particles so, for a hard cheese, the temperature is raised, a process known as scalding. Conversely, the temperature is kept lower for soft cheeses. High temperatures tend to give a hard rubbery curd, while low temperatures will give a soft, jelly-like curd.

The mass of curds and whey will be cut by special knives; for hard cheeses the cutting will be very fine to release even more whey, for soft cheeses the curd is hardly cut at all. Then the whey is drawn off leaving just the curds.

Timing and temperature is critical throughout and it is largely the combination of these two factors which is one of the biggest factors determining the many different styles of cheese.

For hard cheeses, the curd is now broken up into small pieces, known as milling, and salt is added to act as a preservative and flavour enhancer, before the curd is placed in the moulds. For soft cheeses, the curd will be gently ladled into the moulds, disturbing it as little as possible.

Once in the moulds, the curd will be left to drain naturally for soft cheeses and pressed to expel still more whey for hard cheeses.

The final stage is ripening or maturing and it is during this stage that the character of a cheese really starts to develop. Until now most cheeses are little more than lumps of pale curd; wetter or drier certainly but seldom with very much flavour. As the cheese starts to ripen, the flavour starts to develop, the rind starts to form, the blue or white moulds start to grow and the cheese starts to take on its visual, aromatic and gastronomic character. Some cheeses ripen from the inside out (Stilton, Cheddar, Beaufort) whereas others ripen from the outside, with the centre being the last to ripen (Brie, St Marcellin, Epoisses). Soft cheeses ripen quite quickly and are generally ready to eat within a few weeks. Hard cheeses mature more slowly taking anything from a few months to three years or more for extra hard cheeses like Parmigiano Reggiano.

## ❖ Cheese rinds

A rind is an integral part of any cheese, except for the very freshest, or one which has been artificially prevented from forming a rind by, for instance, immersing in brine or wrapping in something which prevents or restricts the air getting to the cheese; for example wax, or plastic vacuum bags. Rindless cheeses include Feta and some blue cheeses, such as Roquefort, which are wrapped in foil. Such examples can be pretty good, but generally rindless cheese is less interesting. A common reason for preventing the formation of a rind is to maintain the moisture content of the cheese and thus keep the price of the cheese low.

Most cheese rinds are simply a hardened bit of the cheese, caused by the curd drying out. This is either completely natural or encouraged by encasing in a bandage of cheese cloth, or rubbing the outer surface of the cheese with salt, brine, butter or olive oil. Other rinds result from the formation of benign moulds. These are known as 'Bloomy Rind' cheeses or 'Croûte Fleuri' in French. They include Brie and Camembert. Still another style of cheese is the 'Washed Rind' family where the outer surface of the cheese is washed or brushed with a liquid such as brine, wine, beer or brandy, to encourage the growth of a benign bacterium, B.Linens. These cheeses are usually easily distinguishable by their russet/terracotta coloured rinds and pungent smell.

So, most cheeses are likely to have rinds and the question arises: Which rinds should I eat? I know people who will cut the rind off every cheese, and others who eat all rinds. The rind always has a different texture and flavour to the interior of the cheese and whether you eat the rind or not should be determined principally by whether you find the rind enhances, or detracts from, your enjoyment of the cheese. It's as simple as that.

Personally, I tend to side with the great Pierre Androuet who recommended removing the rind on most cheeses. I certainly would not recommend eating the rind of a cheese which has not been covered in transit.

## ❖ Organic Cheeses

Mary Langman was one of the small band of people who, with Eve Balfour at their head, established The Soil Association in 1946. I know Mary as the sister of Elizabeth Montgomery of Cheddar cheese fame. Now Montgomery Cheddar is not organic but it most certainly is made in the spirit of 'Healthy soil, healthy plants, healthy people' which Eve Balfour put at the centre of her philosophy. With today's penchant for everything to be enumerated, authenticated and certified, organic foods have, I think, in some ways, taken a wrong turning. The idea of flying in beans from Kenya bearing an organic label would, I suspect, be an anathema to Eve Balfour. Cheeses such as Montgomery, produced according to long established principles and relatively locally, would be much more up her street.

Most of the best cheeses are made on a small scale using non-intensive methods in harmony with nature; but not many of them have ticked all the boxes and gone through the full certification process. For the main part they have not done this because cheesemakers and bureaucracy are not natural bedfellows. Most of their production methods are organic in all but name; but they are not necessarily able to demonstrate, to the satisfaction of an inspector, that they have followed all the rules all of the time. So here, perhaps, we have the answer as to why not many of the best cheeses are certified organic.

"But," I hear you say, "I can find organic cheeses in supermarkets." Yes you can but, with a few honourable exceptions, these organic cheeses are so labelled more for marketing reasons than for any gain in quality. A large cheese factory will buy in organic milk which is probably of high quality and which should, in theory, result in a better quality cheese. But all too often the large factory, because it needs large sales volumes to survive, produces a bland cheese which does not prove too challenging for consumers.

There are one or two really good cheeses which are also organic; Daylesford, until January 2006 made by Joe Schneider, is a supreme example. Joe is a great cheesemaker but I really believe his cheese would not be so wonderfully complex if he did not use organic milk of the highest quality. You only have to taste the liquid milk to realise that it is something very different from your average pinta.

So yes, I would certainly like to see more of the better producers going organic. I believe in organic principles but, as with so many things, the rules need to be simplified for the smaller producers. Perhaps then we would see more truly outstanding organic cheeses. But, in the meantime, please don't let the fact that a cheese is not organic put you off from buying it.

# A STINKER FROM DIJON

## ❖ Epoisses: Jean Berthaut

To lunch at La Pomme d'Or with Jean Berthaut and there I heard his story.

As a boy, just after the Second World War, he watched his father struggle to establish his cheesemaking business. The war had decimated production of Epoisses. At the turn of the century there were 300 farms producing Epoisses. In 1945 there were just two. Jean's father, Robert, had a dream; to recreate the cheese he remembered enjoying, that his grandmother made.

Robert laboured hard, ridiculed by his neighbours for his old fashioned ways. They all had big new tractors; what was Robert doing, messing around with a few smelly cheeses? Who would buy them? Alfred Le Blanc of La Pomme d'Or was his first customer. There is a photograph of him still, in the restaurant sitting in the chair by the fire where I am sitting now. At first Robert's cheeses were poor and often there were tears in his eyes as he buried his failures in a field at night so the neighbours would not see. But Robert was a Berthaut and determination is in their blood. He went to talk to other grandmothers who knew how to make the cheese; and little by little his cheeses improved.

He established his business and, when Jean returned from military service in 1979, there was a good business for him to develop. Through these years of the 1960's and 1970's Berthaut was the sole producer of true Epoisses. Others were selling cheese they called Epoisses but usually it was not washed in Marc de Bourgogne, nor properly matured. Robert applied for Appellation Contrôlée status in 1965 in an attempt to ensure that standards were maintained. He was refused because he was the only producer. However, Appellation Contrôlée status was finally granted in 1991 and now there are three other producers.

Berthaut is still the largest, making over half of all the Epoisses produced each year. In addition there is Fromagerie Gaugry, who moved into new premises in 2004; the old Pastis Ricard building on the N74 at Gevrey Chambertin. And there is Fromagerie Germain, now owned by the giant Triballat, and a single farmhouse producer, Marroniers. Between them, these four firms make nearly 2½ million cheeses each year and consumption is increasing by 10%.

And what of the history of Epoisses? The village grew up around an ancient fortress with double fortification, in a strategically important position on the route between Dijon and Paris. Strategically important but built in the middle of a plain and not naturally an easily defended site. Inside the fortifications are 15th century houses and a rare dovecote containing 3000 nesting holes as well as a 13th century church. In the 16th century a Cistercian religious community was established at Epoisses which, it is said, brought with it the recipe for Epoisses. When they left in the 18th century, the farmers took over production. It was during the period 1775 to 1914 that the production methods of Epoisses were really established and documented. There was, however, a lot of individuality, with over 300 farms producing more Epoisses than is made nowadays. The after-effects of the First and Second World Wars almost destroyed production of the cheese. Farmers were not interested when there were plenty of alternatives, such as cereal cultivation, which were much easier and which were encouraged by the authorities in order to ensure self-sufficiency after the deprivations of wartime. Which brings us to Robert Berthaut and his determination which brought about the renaissance of the cheese.

Not content with resting on laurels others might consider sufficient, Jean Berthaut shows a determination almost equal to his father's. Jean had noticed gradual changes in the milk he was receiving from the 33 farms which send him their milk. It was losing its character, losing its flavour, becoming more bland and was, in Jean's words, "simply like a chemical." He put this down to the fact that farmers were changing to Friesian/Holstein cows, the ubiquitous black and whites that each produce 14,000 litres per year. So Jean pushed for a change to the appellation regulations and, after a five-year year changeover period, the milk will have to come from just 3 breeds: Brune, Montbéliarde and Simmental. These breeds typically produce less than two thirds of the volume of the Friesian/Holstein cows, but the milk is much richer and more full-flavoured.

Another decision Jean had to make concerned pasteurisation. In the late 1990's Jean could not be sure of the quality of all the milk he was receiving. Apart from changing the breed of their cows, some farmers had allowed hygiene standards to drop. The answer, of course, was to improve hygiene standards but this would take time. Jean could not risk problems with his cheese so, reluctantly, he took the decision to pasteurise the milk.

With the change back to traditional breeds, the lower yields and an increased awareness of the need for good hygiene, milk standards are improving and I discussed with Jean my hopes that he might return to making his cheese from raw milk. He feels that now he could do this, but he would lose his new market in America which does not permit raw milk cheeses less than 90 days old. He also believes that pasteurisation may be necessary for him, not to ensure the milk is safe, but to prove to the authorities that it is safe. It is sad to think that commerce and regulation are depriving us of cheeses which I feel might be even more interesting and certainly more complex.

Making the cheese is slow and complicated. The benign bacterium, B.Linens, is added to the milk which is kept in a vat overnight. The following morning the milk is transferred into rectangular 'buckets' where the curds form very slowly over a period of about 16 hours, because little or no coagulant is used. This ensures that the finished cheese is moist and creamy with a fine texture. When the curd has formed sufficiently, it is ladled, by hand, into the moulds where it is allowed to drain naturally for a further day. Once out of the moulds, the cheeses are sprinkled lightly with salt and then left to dry further in special drying rooms, before finally reaching the affinage, or ripening, rooms. Here they ripen for at least three weeks, often longer, during which time each cheese is washed by hand three times each week with a brine solution which is progressively enriched with Marc de Bourgogne. It is this washing process combined with the bacterium, B.Linens, which was added to the milk, which is responsible for the russet colour of the rind and, to a very large extent, determines the style of the cheeses because it affects the way the cheese proteins break down.

The rind of the finished cheese is smooth, almost glossy, and a slightly cloudy golden russet colour. Its rind also offers an initial experience of the penetrating, spirituous smell of the cheese. It is a real stinker! But the amazing thing is that, despite its ferocious aroma, the taste of the cheeses is remarkably well balanced, with beautiful rich and rounded savoury flavours. The inside of the cheese is a pale, ivory colour, perhaps with hints of terracotta. Nowadays it is almost invariably sold in small wooden cylindrical boxes that hold together the cheese, which otherwise can be very runny. It is a small flat disc about 10 cm in diameter and 4 cm in height which ripens from the rind inwards. The Parisians like Epoisses creamy right to the centre but Jean Berthaut says he likes it best when 1/3rd of the cheese remains firm at the centre. For Jean, the ideal age of his cheese is six weeks from the date it was made. When I tasted cheeses of various ages with Jean, it was apparent that during the first four weeks the cheese changes little. It is the final weeks or even days which are critical when the true, glorious character of the cheese is revealed with its noble, tangy, fruity flavour.

The intense, rich flavour of Epoisses demands in any accompanying food, either a plain flavour, which it can overwhelm, or an equally rich flavour with which it can play on equal terms. The former is typified by new potatoes, simply boiled, with Epoisses gently melted over them, much as one would serve Raclette. Perhaps add a little finely chopped sorrel, or even cumin, to the Epoisses during melting. The texture of the potatoes is a wonderful foil to the Epoisses and there is absolutely no clash of flavours, the Epoisses winning hands down. For a more substantial meal there is little better to partner Epoisses than a steak of Charolais beef. Cook the steak to your choice and again, gently melt the Epoisses over the meat. In both cases make certain that the cheese is not bubbly or over heated – just simply and gently melted in a warm oven. Serious pleasure awaits you.

### ❖ Other full, pungent cheeses

Ami Chambertin is almost identical to Epoisses, but is a brand made exclusively by the firm of Gaugry, just outside the village of Gevrey Chambertin in Burgundy.

Carré de l'Est is made in a two styles, which is confusing; one is a bloomy rind, like Camembert, and the other is a washed rind like Epoisses. The latter is the more distinctive and worthwhile. Made in eastern France, it has a full, powerful flavour and can be quite salty.

Celtic Promise is an interesting cheese, which has won Supreme Champion at The British Cheese Awards. It is made by a Dutchman, John Savage-Onstwedder, in west Wales and has quite a firm texture, not unlike a young Gouda, but the rind is then washed in cider which gives it a much fuller flavour.

Although similar to Epoisses, to me Langres always has the hint of a fine grain texture, which is never quite lost no matter how mature. The flavour is more sour milk than Epoisses but lasts wonderfully. It is made near the town of the same name north of Dijon.

Livarot is one of the great cheeses of Normandy. Easily recognisable by the five circles of raffia, which encircle it and which gave it it's nickname of Le Petit Colonel (after the five stripes of a French colonel). Firm though yielding in texture, it often has a few tiny holes. The flavour is complex and lingering.

Pont L'Evêque, also from Normandy, is very similar to Livarot but in a square shape and thinner, which makes it more likely to dry out and consequently more difficult to find in good condition.

Maroilles, originally a monastery cheese from the north of France, can be very powerful, I would say overpowering; but, when good, it has an appealing bitter/sweet balance.

Munster is another monastery cheese; indeed the name Munster is derived from monastery. From Alsace in eastern France, it has an assertive flavour, rich and sweetly herby. Very similar to Epoisses.

One might assume that Stinking Bishop is also a monastery cheese but, in fact, it is a recent invention of Charles Martell who makes the cheese in western Gloucestershire. The name derives from an ancient variety of pear. The pear juice is fermented into perry, which is then used to wash the rind of the cheese. The result is similar to Epoisses.

Tornegus is another recent invention, by the late James Aldridge, and is a young Caerphilly cheese, which is washed in a mixture of brine, white wine and herbs. It has a full aroma and quite a powerful flavour. The texture softens from that of Caerphilly but nonetheless remains firmer than most washed rind cheeses.

Less powerful in flavour is Reblochon, made in the alpine Savoie region of eastern France, from the milk of Tarentaise cows and possessing the most marvellous soft texture reminiscent of melting chocolate. The flavour is quite delicate and herby.

Ardrahan from western Ireland has a full, earthy flavour, above all savoury and nutty.

Mont des Cats is a monastery cheese produced by Trappiste monks at the Abbey of Bailleul. It has a smooth texture and a delightful, mild flavour.

Durrus is made by Jeffa Gill just outside Bantry in western Ireland and is notable for its superb texture, not unlike Reblochon, and a delightful, herby yet fruity flavour. At its best it is a stunning cheese.

Gubbeen is another of County Cork's treasures. Made by Giana Ferguson, it has a slightly firmer texture than many of these cheeses, and a buttery flavour.

St Nectaire is made in the heart of the beautiful Auvergne region of central France. With its mushroomy aroma and unctuous texture it is stunning when eaten young from a good farmhouse producer. Unfortunately there are too many unimpressive factory versions.

Taleggio, at its best, is a real stunner from northern Italy. With its smooth, melt-in-the-mouth texture, it has a fruity almost aromatic flavour.

## ❖ Pinot Gris Vendange Tardive 1997: Kuentz-Bas

Jean Berthaut recommends a good Chablis to enjoy with his Epoisses. The Chablis vineyards are, after all, only some 25 miles away and certainly Chablis cuts through the creaminess of Epoisses to very good effect. Another possibility is a red Burgundy such as Savigny-Les-Beaune. The mayors of Savigny-Les-Beaune and Epoisses came together in August 1962 and solemnly declared the 'marriage' of their respective cheese and wine, recording in beautiful manuscript that they should for ever after remain inseparable on the tables of France.

But to me, Epoisses all too easily overwhelms any Burgundy, red or white. It was Lyonel Lecomte who first got me thinking about an Alsace Pinot Gris Vendange Tardive as the perfect foil for this powerful, pungent cheese. And indeed it works – very well. The wine I found ideal was from Maison Kuentz-Bas and their vineyards 8 km south of Colmar.

In 1975, Rachel (not then my wife but soon to be) and I arrived at Kuentz-Bas a week early for the harvest, which we were due to pick. But no matter, we were given a charming little room above some outbuildings and told to 'faire le tourisme'. And what a charming region it is. Kuentz-Bas trace their origins back to 1795 when Joseph Kuentz founded the business. In 1918 the Bas family married into the business, bringing with them their own vineyards, and the name of the business was changed to Kuentz-Bas to reflect the new partnership, which lasted until 2001 when there was a parting of the ways and the firm was taken over. Christian Bas remains, as ever, a firm advocate of the wines which bear his name. They are to be found in Husseren-Les-Châteaux, nestled in the foothills of the Vosges Mountains, overlooking the wide plain of the Rhine to the Black Forest, on the far side of the river, in Germany. We drove out most days in our MGB to visit Colmar, Strasbourg and many of the small villages; or just to drive through the vineyards, which reach an altitude of nearly 400 metres.

Then it was into the full swing of the harvest. The weather was far from perfect and the harvest was difficult. Not one to be remembered, except by us vendangeurs, setting out each morning often in thick, cool, damp fog; by the time we reached the vineyards we were above the fog and could look down on it in the valley below, with just the occasional church spire rising through it. A pig was killed to feed us and every evening we all ate together in convivial company. It was a great time – very friendly and sociable.

Recently Christian Bas was kind enough to send me a bottle of his Pinot Gris

Cuvée Caroline Vendange Tardive 1997. It was superb. Produced from grapes which were over-ripe when picked and with concentrated sugar levels, it is a wine of substance and intensity but retains a very appealing freshness. Bright straw yellow in colour, with appealing flashes of green, and a fine aromatic bouquet, with pineappley fruit and hints of bacon. It is sufficiently rich and full-bodied to stand up to the Epoisses and, although I would guess the acidity is fairly low, it is there in sufficient quantity to cut through the creaminess of the cheese. The flavour is delicately smoky with hints of apricot and fresh pineapple fruit. The touch of sweetness in the wine balances the salt of the cheese to great effect.

Christian Bas recalls "In 1997, I remember that we had splendid botrytis on the berries due to alternating sunshine and humidity". The grapes for this wine were picked on 17th November, a full month after the rest of the harvest. It is a risky practice, because if the weather turns bad, as it did when we were picking in 1975, the whole crop can be lost. But in 1997 the weather remained dry until early November resulting in sound, fully ripe grapes which were dried rather than being affected by 'pourriture noble' or noble rot. Nonetheless they had some of the highest sugar levels ever recorded. 1997 is widely regarded as one of the finest vintages in Alsace, comparable to the legendary 1949's and 1959's. Christian expects the Pinot Gris to continue to develop, not reaching its peak until some time around 2015.

Alsace wines are immensely appealing but you need to find the right occasion and the right food to go with them. Epoisses is certainly one successful partner but do not stop there. Other Alsace wines, such as Gewurztraminer Selection des Grains Noble, partner blue cheeses to perfection and many Alsace wines need no food and are superb wines to enjoy simply on their own.

## ❖ Fat content of cheeses

People sometimes think that a cheese like Epoisses is going to be full of fat. They are put off by some labels which say 45% fat or even 70% fat. But these labels refer to the fat as a percentage of the dry matter in the cheese. Those with a high moisture content will actually have less fat than drier cheeses. The true percentage of the cheese's weight represented by fat is generally about 20% for soft cheeses and 40% for hard cheeses. The reason cheese is labelled in this, apparently misleading, way is that the moisture content diminishes with age and, if the fat were expressed as a percentage of the total weight, the figure on the label would need to be changed as the cheese matured.

These days we see more 'low fat' cheeses on sale. Sometimes these labels are misleading because who determines what is 'low fat'? Of equal concern is the fact that, if they are genuinely low fat, many of the flavour giving proteins will also have been removed. This results in a cheese with little flavour and little body, which is less satisfying than a full-flavoured, full fat cheese and so one naturally eats more of it.

If you need to watch your fat intake, but still want to enjoy the pleasures of cheese, my advice is to buy a full-flavoured cheese and, because it is so satisfying, you will almost certainly eat less of it and your fat intake will in fact be lower.

Research by two notable French scientists suggests that only a limited amount of the fatty acids in cheese is actually absorbed into the body; most is passed straight with the calcium, which the body cannot absorb at such high levels as are present in cheese, especially unpasteurised cheeses.

THE QUINTESSENTIAL BRITISH CHEESE

## ❖ Montgomery's Cheddar

From the reputed site of Camelot, a hill fort near South Cadbury, one can just make out the cows grazing the rich silty-clay loam pastures on the Montgomery's Manor Farm at North Cadbury. The black and white Friesians graze contentedly, seemingly unaware of James and Archie Montgomery's intense interest in their diet — an interest dictated by the fact that what the cows eat has a direct influence on the milk they produce and thus the cheese. As a cheesemonger I visited Jamie every couple of months to select which days' cheeses we would buy, and the variation from one day to the next never ceased to amaze me. Part of the variation is due to the starter culture they use but the diet of the cows is also critical. On one of my visits I tasted three days' production, which had some distinctly odd flavours which I didn't like. "This is unlike your usual cheese" I said to Jamie. "Mmm" he said, "Those three days the spring ran dry and we had to ration the cows drinking. We thought we'd compensated for this in making the cheese, but obviously we didn't!"

Archie & Jamie also believe in strip grazing, where the cows eat all the grass in a small area of a field before being allowed to graze the rest of the field. The idea is that, if they were allowed access to the whole field, they would eat just the lush top of the grass first, before getting down to the higher fibre base of the grass; cheese produced from the top of the grass would lack body and that produced from the bottom of the grass would lack protein.

Jamie is equally focused on the cheesemaking process, and particularly the reasons for variation in the cheeses. He keeps detailed notes of each day's production and refers to these when tasting the cheeses 6, 9, 12 or 15 months later. From this, he builds up a picture of what produces a successful cheese and what might not be so good. Now and then, he might make a minor adjustment to current practice if he feels that it will result in more superb cheeses or fewer bad ones. He says there was too much variation in the past, and now he hopes to produce superb cheeses more consistently. Overall, the cheddar-making process at Montgomery's has changed little over the years and the cheese today is probably little different from the cheese produced in past centuries, just more consistently good.

Jamie has identified a number of factors that are responsible for the quality of his cheese and they are:

The region in which it is made, the county of Somerset in South West England, has a climate and geology which provides lush pastures, enabling the cows to produce milk which is perfect for cheddar cheese. Jamie only uses the milk provided by the farm's own cows and, by deciding himself on their grazing and diet, he can influence the quality and character of the milk; so that he gets just the flavours he is looking for. When it comes to the cheesemaking, he uses raw milk to preserve all the natural flavours of the milk and increase the complexity of his cheese. Jamie is equally exacting about the starter culture he uses, insisting on the traditional live bacteria provided by 'pint starters'. He uses seven different cultures, one for each day of the week, and each imparts a slightly different flavour to the cheese. Not for Jamie the current vogue of vegetarian rennet. He insists on using animal rennet because he believes it is more holistic and gives a more rounded flavour.

Cheddaring, which consists of cutting the curd into blocks and repeatedly piling the blocks on top of one another so that the texture changes from crumbly lumps to pliable, elastic slabs, is done by hand to give the superb friable texture that is a characteristic of his cheese.

Much cheddar is vacuum packed in plastic but Jamie sticks to the traditional cloth binding which enables the cheese to breathe during its long, slow maturation of up to 18 months which allows time for the potential flavours in the cheese to develop.

In association with Slow Food, the international organisation which helps preserve and promote the enjoyment and importance of food, and together with two other local cheesemakers, he has devised a protocol incorporating the above procedures, which is now followed by all three farms. As a result, their cheese is entitled to the designation 'Artisan Somerset Cheddar'. The protocol does not attempt to standardise the production of the three farms, and the cheeses of each are recognisably different. However, following the principles of the protocol sets the cheeses above the quality of the mass of inferior cheeses which carry, yet have debased, the cheddar name and also above even the other farmhouse cheesemakers in the region.

Montgomery's Cheddar is full-flavoured and slow-maturing. Although the potential of each cheese is apparent at about 6 or 7 months of age when I would first taste them, it is not until 12 months of age that the flavour really starts to develop. In my view, the best cheeses should be kept until at least 18 months of age. By this age the cheese has developed a unique depth and complexity of flavour. The flavour is strong but, unlike some lesser cheddars, not overpowering. The intricate blend of flavours − sweet fruit (peaches mainly), nuts, grass, herbs, caramel and a whole host more − creates a truly exceptional cheese. The depth of flavour lasts and lasts in the mouth. The texture, too, is superb. Not the rather oily, moist texture of most mass-produced cheddars but a dry, almost grainy, texture which encourages nibbling rather than devouring. If you're looking for a cheddar which blasts your taste buds, Montgomery is not for you. If you're looking for a cheddar with sublime complexity, look no further − you have found it.

## ❖ Other hard farmhouse cheeses

Other great makers of cheddar are Keen's, which I find is slightly more steely and less fruity than Montgomery's, and Westcombe, which is beginning to show great style, more creamy than either Keen's or Montgomery's.

Amongst my other favourite hard English cheeses are Double Gloucester, especially that produced by Jonathan Crump at Wick Court, overlooking a bend in the Severn, some 10 miles south east of Gloucester. To approach Wick Court is like stepping back to the 1950's. A delightfully ramshackle farmyard is home to pigs, sheep and chickens as well as the Gloucester cows which produce the milk for the cheese. Jonathan is dedicated to all of them. Gloucester cows are now rare but time was when all Gloucester cheese was made from their milk. The resulting cheese has a golden colour, with a smoother, silkier texture than Cheddar. The flavour is full yet soft and rounded, but with an attractive piquancy.

Jonathan also produces a Single Gloucester (made from partly skimmed milk whereas the double uses full cream milk) but I actually prefer the Single Gloucester made by Charles Martell a few miles away. It has a lovely, fresh, spring-like quality.

There are a number of cheddar-style cheeses made on farms across the country, but generally sold under the name of the farm rather than under the cheddar name which, in my view, should only apply to cheeses made in the south west of England. Amongst the best are Daylesford Organic, until recently made by Joe Schneider in Gloucestershire. Joe is one of the best cheesemakers I know and he has produced some stunning cheeses full of flavour, yet with an enticing delicacy and lightness.

Another excellent example is Lincolnshire Poacher, made since 1992 with great success by Simon Read in Lincolnshire.

## ❖ Classic Claret for a classic cheese: Château La Garde

While I suppose I must concede that the natural partner to Cheddar is cider - after all, the apples are, or were, grown in vast quantities in orchards alongside the pastures where the cows graze – I must confess to never having found a cider which I really liked. At lunchtime I enjoy a good real ale, such as Wadworth's 6X, with Montgomery's cheddar but for more refined pleasure I look towards Bordeaux.

The wines of Bordeaux are, I suppose, those to which many winemakers and wine drinkers aspire. The region has the reputation of producing the world's best wines and, even now, with good wine being produced all over the place, few would argue that truly exceptional wines come from Bordeaux. Even lower down the scale, there are some remarkably good wines produced in this area of western France; wines known for centuries to British customers as Claret.

Within the Bordeaux region are sub-regions; Médoc, Graves, St Emilion, Pomerol, Sauternes and Barsac, together with other lesser areas. Within these sub regions are Villages and within the Villages are the Châteaux. It is important to know your way around all these, in order to choose wines with which one will be pleased – not always easy.

The grape varieties, by contrast are easy; red wines are made from blends of Cabernet Sauvignon and Merlot, with smaller quantities of Cabernet Franc and Petit Verdot. White wines are made from Sauvignon Blanc and Semillon. Sauternes and Barsac produce sweet wines; the other areas generally produce dry wines. However it is worth checking before buying, as it is not always obvious from the label.

The Médoc is generally regarded as the top sub region, mainly because it houses the largest number of the great Châteaux. But St Emilion and Pomerol also produce top class wines and, of course, there are the great sweet wines of Sauternes and Barsac. So it is really only Graves that historically might have been considered the poor relation but, even here, one cannot discount such great wines as Château Haut Brion. Over the last decade or so, the quality level at a number of Châteaux has improved markedly, putting the area back up with the Médoc, with which it shares a similar gravely soil.

Because the wines of Bordeaux are complex and subtle, some people now pass them over in favour of more immediately appealing wines from the New World. This is a mistake. The best Bordeaux wines are incomparable, and even those lower down the scale offer nuances of flavour and interest which wines produced in more climatically friendly areas seldom achieve.

Top post-war vintages are 2005, 2000, 1990, 1982, 1961 and 1945. Top Villages are Pauillac, Margaux, St Julien and St Estephe. Top Châteaux are Latour, Lafite, Mouton-Rothschild, Margaux, Haut Brion, Yquem, Pétrus – but there are plenty of others. Incidentally, it is always worth looking out for the second wine of great Châteaux. They are generally good and a fraction of the price of the first wine.

During a visit to one of the great Châteaux of Pauillac, Château Mouton-Rothschild, Rachel and I were especially privileged to taste the 1945 in half bottle. Simply amazing. Highly concentrated blackcurrant flavour. Very full, rich and powerful. Magnificent deep ruby colour. To taste it in the cellars in which it was matured, in the middle of the vineyard where it was made, was very special.

But these are the great wines and should, perhaps, be reserved for quiet contemplation by themselves, without the intrusion of food of any type. To accompany Montgomery's cheddar, with its huge flavour, requires a more robust, less ethereal wine. On a number of occasions, I have found that the wines coming from the Graves region, just to the south of Bordeaux, provide enough body and richness to avoid being overpowered by the cheese, whilst at the same time possessing enough finesse and elegance to be interesting in their own right. In particular the Pessac-Leognan area, which actually abuts the city, and includes the famous Château Haut Brion, has some ideal wines.

At a recent tasting I was particularly impressed by Château La Garde 2000. The progress at the Château, since it was acquired by Dourthe in 1990, has been evident and much commented on. The vineyard consists of some 56 hectares planted with 52% Cabernet Sauvignon and 48% Merlot producing an average of some 180,000 bottles a year. There is also a small amount of white wine produced from the Sauvignon grape.

The 2000 was immediately appealing, robust and earthy, with strong base notes, rich and robust yet with concentrated, smooth, ripe fruit and sufficient acidity and minerality to hold it together. Although still young and with much life left in it (I think one could happily drink it in 10 years time), the tannins were not too evident, and it was already very approachable. It is a lovely wine and a near perfect partner for Montgomery's Cheddar.

## ❖ Cheesemaking in Britain

Ever since Roman times, when it is believed the legions took Cheshire cheese back to Rome, Britain has been capable of producing world class cheeses. We may not have been the first to produce cheese; that honour almost certainly goes to somewhere near present day Iran. In all probability the first cheese was the result of an accident. It is believed that a shepherd, carrying milk in his leather bottle, found that it had curdled. This was caused by the natural presence, on the leather, of Rennet, an enzyme found on the lining of calves' stomachs.

Little is known about cheesemaking in Britain until the Norman Conquest when monks, accompanying William the Conqueror, built abbeys and started making cheese as they would have done previously in France. One recipe they almost certainly brought with them was for a cheese like Roquefort, made from sheep's milk and which they made at Jervaulx and Fountains abbeys in Yorkshire. Over the centuries this cheese morphed into Wensleydale.

With the dissolution of the monasteries under Henry VIII in 1534, production of cheese passed to farmers and their wives. In France, cheesemaking remained with the abbeys for another 250 years. As a result, I like to think that British cheeses developed a style which reflected the rural, labouring nature of their production. French cheeses developed a style which reflected the more intellectual nature of the religious communities in which they were produced. British cheeses were designed for sustenance; French cheeses became more a way of admiring the skill of the maker.

The first 'factory' cheese produced in England was made at Derby in 1870. During the Second World War, when cheesemaking was strictly limited as being a poor use of labour and resources, 'National' cheese was produced. Restrictions remained even after the war which meant that few farmers returned to cheesemaking and the dominance of factory cheesemakers meant that little of interest was produced.

In the 1980's there was something of a renaissance of British cheesemaking, with a younger generation reviving old techniques and persuading those who could still remember how real cheese was made, to pass on the recipes and their skills.

Compared with some 1,500 cheesemakers in the 1930's, today, about 350 cheesemakers produce about 400,000 tons of cheese each year. Of these producers, two thirds make less than 50 tons, so the industry is still dominated by large factories. Another dominating factor is that 60% of the cheese produced is cheddar! Most of us are hardly adventurous, but there are increasing signs that this is changing and those producing the best quality cheeses are selling all they can make.

## ❖ The British Embassy, Paris

In 1997 Lady Jay, the wife of our then Ambassador, Sir Michael Jay, invited me to attend a tasting of British Cheeses at the embassy in Paris. While in Paris she used all the embassy dinners and receptions to promote British foods; a tough job, which she did exceptionally well. Her natural charm gets her a long way but beneath the charm is a steely determination that British food should stand alongside, or above, French food in terms of quality.

The history of the place is humbling. It was built by the duc de Charost between 1720 and 1723, visited by Napoleon Bonaparte (his sister owned the house), bought by The Duke of Wellington on behalf of George III in 1814 and was the venue for many a sparkling evening under the legendary ambassadorship of Duff Cooper.

The array of British cheeses on display at the tasting that night was impressive enough to draw gasps of admiration from the assembled French food professionals and journalists. They really could not believe that Britain produced such good cheeses – it was outside their orbit and their experience. Despite this, sales of British cheeses in France remain sporadic, largely because most of the good cheeses are produced by small one or two-man businesses which simply don't have the resources (or inclination) to export. But at least Lady Jay drew praise from the French, which is an achievement in itself.

After the tasting we sat down for dinner in the Tapestry Dining Room. 'We' was Sir Michael and Lady Jay, Richard Codrington and his wife, Michel Roux and I. Michel regaled us with stories of his time working in the kitchens of the embassy. He was writing his autobiography, 'Life is a Menu', and wanted to revisit the kitchens. He said that nothing had changed in 50 years!

## ❖ My Star British Cheesemakers

The renaissance in artisan British cheesemaking has thrown up some stars, who either make the cheese themselves or, in some cases, oversee the quality though without necessarily making the cheese every day. In no particular order, I would number the following amongst the very best in my roll of honour:

| | |
|---|---|
| Jamie Montgomery | Montgomery's Cheddar |
| Mary Quicke | Quicke's Cheddar |
| Simon Jones | Lincolnshire Poacher |
| Joe Schneider | Daylesford Organic |
| Barry Graham | Loch Arthur |
| Ruth Kirkham | Kirkham's Lancashire |
| Edward & Christine Appleby | Appleby's Cheshire |
| Jonathan Crump | Double Gloucester |
| Charles Martell | Single Gloucester & Stinking Bishop |
| Leon Downey | Llangloffan |
| John Savage | Teifi |
| Pam Rodway | Carola |
| Charlie Westhead | Finn & Perroche |
| Anne Wigmore | Waterloo & Wigmore |
| Debbie Mumford | Sharpham |
| Pat Aldridge | Tornegus & Celtic Promise |
| Alison & Kevin Blunt | Golden Cross |
| Mary Holbrook | Tymsboro |
| Robin Congdon | Beenleigh Blue & Ticklemore |
| Ian Skailles | Cropwell Bishop Stilton |
| Richard Rowlett | Colston Bassett Stilton |
| Margaret Mar | Albion & Delicatus |
| Stella Bennett | Innes Button |
| Stephen Fletcher | Berkswell |

# THE CISTERCIANS: CHEESE'S GREAT BENEFACTORS

### ❖ Abbaye Notre Dame de Cîteaux

Few cheeses have a better claim than Cîteaux in bringing together the two threads of this book — cheese and wine, nor to represent more explicitly the intimate historical connection between the making of cheese and religious communities. Le Fromage de Cîteaux, therefore, holds a very special place amongst all cheeses for its symbolism; and yet that would not be enough were it not also a simply wonderful cheese.

A religious community was first established at Cîteaux in March 1098, when Abbot Robert, and several monks, left the Benedictine abbey at Molesme and settled in the woods some 15 miles south of Dijon and 100 miles from Molesme. Their motivation for leaving was a desire to rekindle the principles of St Benedict which, they felt, were no longer followed at Molesme. By their actions they established the Cistercian order, named after their first small church at Cîteaux. From the beginning, their motto was "*Ora et Labora*", "Pray and Work"; as Frère Placide told me "looking after their herd of cows was central to the founding principles of the monastery".

Also central to their needs was wine, both for meals and for use during holy offices. The land around Cîteaux was not suitable for wines but, 10 miles to the west, they discovered ideal conditions where generous benefactors allowed them to acquire land, plant vines and, in 1116, construct buildings for vinification and cellaring. That land was Clos de Vougeot, now one of Burgundy's most famous and greatest vineyards.

The centuries passed and the monks of Cîteaux continued to make both cheese and wine until the French revolution when, on 13th February 1790, both the abbey and Clos de Vougeot were declared state property and the monks were forced to leave their beloved Cîteaux. They returned to their abbey after more than 100 years and cheesemaking resumed in 1907, but Clos de Vougeot had been sold and was never returned to the monks.

Frère Placide has known the cheese for over 30 years and says that it was being made twice a day in the 1930's enabling the milk to be used fresh from the cow. With modern refrigeration the brothers can store the milk and now make cheese twice a week, on Mondays and Thursdays. As far as I know, they are the only abbey where all the milk for cheesemaking still comes from their own cows. Frère Jean-Claude explained to me that they look after 150 Montbéliard cows, of which 70 or so are in milk at any one time, producing 500,000 litres of milk each year; enough to make 2,000 cheeses each week. He says that in the 1920's the cheese was hard, a little like Gruyère but that the brothers then decided to change to a recipe similar to the one used at L'Abbaye de Notre Dame de Port du Salut. It was a wise decision because the present cheese is superb.

Three of the brothers make the cheese, which takes three hours from start to finish. They raise the temperature of the milk to 33˚c, add rennet and the curd forms in half to three quarters of an hour. It is then cut and stirred for a further half hour and then drained. It is then moulded and lightly pressed overnight. The following morning the brothers immerse the cheeses in brine for 4 to 5 hours. Affinage, during which the cheeses are washed in brine and turned daily, takes about 3 weeks at 12˚c before it is ready to eat.

At first appearance Cîteaux resembles a cross between Reblochon and Port Salut but it is, in reality, a unique cheese in its own right. They are discs of about 17 cm diameter and 4 cm high, weighing approx 750g. Initially the aroma is pungent in the extreme. You may wonder what you have bought. But, unwrapped for a little while, the aroma disperses. Unlike some cheese aficionados who like the crust of the cheese, I would recommend that you cut off the rind of Cîteaux because I find it detracts from the sublime pleasure of the paste. To me the rind is too crunchy and too intense in flavour. The texture of the paste is a delight; soft, supple and yielding, slightly firmer than melting chocolate; but it is the flavour, which is its stunning feature. There is just so much of it: herby, spicy, fruity with hints of hazelnuts and hay and a pronounced tang. It may be milder than other washed-rind cheeses, such as Epoisses, but the fact that the flavours are mild does not stop there being lots of them. It is a cheese of nuances not a blockbuster; it deserves to be savoured slowly to fully appreciate its character and complexity.

The production of 2,000 cheeses a week is clearly surplus to the needs of the 35 brothers at the abbey but is not nearly sufficient to meet public demand. All the cheese is sold locally and buyers are obliged to collect from the abbey. The result is that nearly all the cheese is consumed locally, although a little makes its way to top Parisian restaurants, and it is extremely difficult to find. Even at the abbey, the brothers often have no cheese for sale.

## ❖ Other monastery-style cheeses

Cîteaux may be one of the few abbeys still to produce cheese entirely from the milk of their own cows but there are plenty of other religious communities who produce cheese and plenty of individuals and companies who produce cheeses of a similar style. This is hardly surprising as monasteries historically were often the centres of expertise in all sorts of matters, not least agricultural and epicurean. They generally enjoyed a high standard of living and entertained visitors to whom they would wish to serve meals of a high quality; so it is natural that they should be the source of many of our present day cheeses.

Monastery cheeses tend to be soft cheeses with a pliable, satiny smooth texture and a washed rind, and are similar to cheeses such as Epoisses. I have referred to most of my favourites in the chapter, 'A Stinker from Dijon'. I draw a distinction between soft cheeses like Brie and smooth cheeses like Cîteaux, although I admit the distinction is subjective and sometimes very hard to put into words. I think what I am trying to say is that the smooth ones are firmer in texture and definitely hold their own shape whereas the soft ones can run once ripe. The smooth ones tend to be lightly pressed, whereas the soft ones are not pressed. As always it is fiendishly difficult to categorise cheeses.

## ❖ A word about additives

There is a noble tradition of adding ingredients to cheese: cumin to Gouda reminding us of the Dutch trading links with the far east, medicinal herbs added by monks to their cheeses, carrot juice to give a richer colour, extra cream to make a particularly succulent cheese. And, of course, some ingredients are essential to cheesemaking; Salt (added to curd for Cheddar, rubbed into the rind for Parmigiano Reggiano) acts as a preservative slowing bacteria growth, dehydrating and enhancing the flavour.

But this tradition has been hijacked by modern marketing methods and some of the additions nowadays are quite horrendous; whoever thought of adding chocolate or Christmas Pudding?

Traditionally ingredients would have been added as part of the cheesemaking process but, all too often these days, plain cheese of poor quality, or with some defect, is minced and then reconstituted with the ingredients added. The result is a pappy texture and a flavour, which does no favours to either the original cheese or the ingredients. My advice: stay clear of cheeses with additives.

## ❖ Burgundy

During my vineyard work experience, my digs in Burgundy were even more basic than in Champagne, but perhaps more charming. I was in a sort of loft above a store in the small village of Ladoix-Serrigny, just north of Beaune. I worked in the vineyards, pruning, and in the cellars, racking wine from one barrel to another or bottling. The people at La Reine Pedauque were charming and my French improved slowly, so that we could communicate pretty well.

After a spell in the Loire and Provence and a quick visit to England, I returned with Rachel to Burgundy for the 1975 harvest. We arrived at La Reine Pedauque and were met with astonishment by Denis Santiard. "Your friend is a girl! You told us only a friend and we had thought you meant a man. We had planned your accommodation the same as before but this time with your friend and a Belgian curé who is also here for the vendange. Clearly that will not be possible". Heads were put together and a splendid solution arrived at. The vicar would stay in my old loft and Rachel and I would be welcome to use a huge but unfurnished and somewhat dilapidated apartment above their exhibition cellars in Beaune. Rachel set to and soon had it very homely. We picked grapes all day, which was fun but tiring, especially as the weather was foul – rain most days. Not good for the grapes, and everyone was fearful of a very poor harvest, which indeed it was.

I came to love Burgundy and find it perhaps the most charming vineyard area in France. It is real country, as English people understand it, except that the crops are grapes. Although the vines stretch almost as far as the eye can see, each vineyard is surprisingly small. Before the French Revolution the church owned particularly extensive vineyards in Burgundy and these were seized by the state and sold off to many individuals. By contrast, in Bordeaux, vineyards were often owned by merchants and their lands were not usually forfeited, unless the owners were of the aristocracy or foreign. Add to this seizure of lands the French inheritance laws, which divide land equally between all children, and the result is the multiplicity of ownership now in place. There are some 30,000 growers and over 100 different appellations contrôlées in Burgundy. Some 'vineyards' may be just one or two rows of vines – not that this is apparent to the casual observer; there are few fences or walls to indicate a change of owner.

In Champagne the blender is everything. In Bordeaux the vineyard or Château is everything. Burgundy is a curious mix of the two. Because of the predominantly small size of each vineyard, merchants, or négociants, became established in much the same way as the blenders in Champagne. But whereas in Champagne this was necessary to improve the quality of the wines, in Burgundy it was brought about for commercial reasons (making up marketable quantities) rather than for reasons of quality. Nowadays most merchants produce good wines (it was not always so) but, alongside the merchants are the real stars; the individual growers who sell their excellent wines (with plenty of nuances of flavour between and even within the different appellations) in small quantities at high prices.

One can pay a lot of money for a Burgundy, but the good ones are incomparable; the trick is to find the good ones. They are rare and, of all regions, a little local knowledge is almost essential. After many years I am still scratching the surface. Of course, the great domaines are nearly always superb. Comtes Lafon, De Vogue, Coche Dury and others. But the prices are astronomic. Searching out the less well-known producers who still make excellent wines can be a frustrating experience. Burgundy is a good friend but a fickle one. Sometimes she will amaze you with an overwhelming display of her virtues. At another one can scarcely see why one ever liked her at all. But, when it comes to cheese, her red wines, made from Pinot Noir grapes, are a constant companion.

The grape varieties in Burgundy are relatively straightforward. Chardonnay is grown for all the great whites and Pinot Noir for the all the great reds with Gamay replacing Pinot Noir in Beaujolais. Aligoté is planted sporadically throughout the region, producing what I consider rather inferior white wines.

At the very heart of Burgundy is the Côte d'Or, between Dijon and just south of Beaune, producing what I think are the greatest red and white wines of

Burgundy. To the north is Chablis, with its classically steely white wines. To the south is Beaujolais, with its generally lighter and fruitier red wines made from the Gamay grape. In between lie the Côte Chalonnaise and Maconnais (in my view poor relations to the Côte d'Or, though they won't thank me for saying it).

Pinot Noir as grown in Burgundy is, to my mind, indisputably one of the best red wines to accompany most soft cheeses. Pinot Noir is a frustrating grape to grow, demanding the highest skills in the vineyard and not a little luck. It gives many problems, such as budding early, so it is susceptible to frosts. Its small tight bunches rot easily and yields have to be tightly controlled, as over-production will result in wishy-washy wines; but too low a yield will be totally uneconomic. As a result, it is not widely grown, although many a more adventurous vigneron in both Europe and the New World has tried. Burgundy, where it has been grown for a millennium, remains its true home and it is here that I look for many of the best wines to accompany cheeses.

## ❖ To dinner at Lameloise

As one enters the restaurant from the uninspiring square in Chagny, south of Beaune, the air of refinement envelops and transports one to another world; a world of the quiet enjoyment of fine food, but thankfully not too quiet as is too often the case in many fine restaurants. Lameloise has the happy murmur of friends enjoying themselves. It is busy, even on a Monday. The waiters are welcoming but a little too formal and starched. Why does good food seem to go with formality? I suppose because the only people who can afford such food demand a certain formality.

The most delicious starter; raw salmon, smoked salmon and mi-cuit (or half cooked) salmon enrobed in a spinach soufflé studded with pieces of lobster. This was too good to be true; light, elegant and simply superb. Served with it were little cannelloni filled with whipped crème fraîche flavoured with fennel. The main course was rabbit with mushrooms served with mashed potatoes, which I found a little too heavy. Then, on the cheeseboard, was Cîteaux, where I had been earlier in the day. Finally, a light, fresh, palate-cleansing pear sorbet served with a whole, slightly caramelised pear and pear biscuits.

## ❖ Clos de Vougeot Grand Cru 1998: Domaine René Engel

The obvious wine to accompany Cîteaux cheese is clearly Clos de Vougeot. Although the monks no longer have any connection with the winemaking at Clos de Vougeot, I felt I had to explore the wines in view of their historical links.

The Clos de Vougeot vineyard, in the northern half of the Côte d'Or and planted almost entirely with Pinot Noir, is now split between 80 different growers and, because I wanted to compare the wines of more than one producer, I went along to Berry Bros & Rudd for a special tasting with their Buying Director, Jasper Morris. Jasper has a house in the hills above Clos de Vougeot and spends part of his time there and part in London. He knows Burgundy and its wines in consummate detail.

It was a change for me to be sitting the other side of the table at Berry's, listening to a tutorial rather than conducting it. While more relaxing, I was reminded how much I like to taste at my own pace rather than at a pace determined by someone else; also that to taste in the evening when one is, perhaps, tired (and certainly one's taste buds are jaded) is not nearly so rewarding as tasting in the late morning.

Nevertheless, the tasting was fascinating; six red wines from Clos de Vougeot from six different producers and five different vintages plus a white Clos de Vougeot, which one seldom sees and was delicious. Those early monks at Cîteaux clearly knew a thing or two about winemaking as the land they planted back in 1109, some 10 years after they founded their monastery, is to this day capable of producing wines of world class stature.

The present vineyard is some 51 hectares, about the size one might expect of a Bordeaux Château producing a single wine; but the Clos has over 80 owners producing 80 different wines with an average production per owner of only just over 1,000 bottles. Hence the need to proceed with caution, as is true everywhere in Burgundy. Apart from the skills of each owner, the position of their vines within the Clos is of critical importance. It may seem strange when the whole vineyard is only 51 hectares but it runs from the well drained limestone at the top of the hill, to the heavy muddy frost-trap clay at the bottom, where it is extremely difficult to produce any wine which can live up to its Grand Cru status. Some owners have parcels of vines scattered around the Clos, which makes it even more difficult to predict with any certainty the quality inside the bottle. Tasting experience is the only way to proceed and Jasper talked us through the wines, passing on some of his considerable knowledge.

What was evident is that the variations within the Clos are at least as great as one would find between the Clos and vineyards 10 miles away. The producer is critical; Jasper even went as far as to give the example of two producers each with holdings in Clos de Vougeot and Volnay. By his reckoning there were more common characteristics between the two wines from each producer than there were between either the two Volnay or the two Clos de Vougeot.

Of the wines we tasted, the two I liked best were the 2000 vintage from Domaine René Engel and the 1993 vintage from Domaine Méo-Camuzet; but the latter only once a second bottle had been opened. The first bottle was very lack-lustre and rather disappointing for a wine retailing at nearly £200 a bottle. The second bottle was superb: dense, rich, lots of fruit, typical Pinot Noir, autumnal, leafy. However I felt that the 2000 from René Engel would be a better match for the cheese. In order to verify this I actually tried a 1998 vintage a few days later alongside the cheese.

169

The Clos de Vougeot 1998 Domaine René Engel was initially quite closed, showing a little red fruit flavour, but after about an hour it really opened up and developed those lovely, leafy, vegetal aromas and flavours which are the hallmark of good Pinot Noir. It showed great elegance and finesse with enough power and structure to partner the Cîteaux cheese superbly. The aroma of the cheese initially threatened to overpower the wine, but its flavour was more refined than suggested by the aroma, especially once the rind was removed. The crusty rind was too strong and aggressive for the wine.

The centre of Domaine René Engel is an impressive building near the square in the village of Vosne Romanee. As is traditional in Burgundy, the vats are on the ground floor, the cellar, housing both barrels and bottles, is below, and there is living space on the first floor.

In Clos de Vougeot, their large 1½ hectare parcel of vines, some of which are as much as 80 years old, is ideally situated near the top of the slope just below the Château itself.

Since 1981, the wines of the Domaine were made by Philippe Engel, René's grandson, but tragically he died of a heart attack at the early age of 49 while sailing in Tahiti. He took the decision to bottle all the Domaine's wines in-house and this was achieved in 1988. Before that much had been sold in bulk to merchants. Philippe achieved great things with the Domaine during his stewardship and I wait with interest to see how it will proceed now that it is under the ownership of Francois Pinault of Château Latour in Bordeaux. Hopefully a great future is assured.

WEARY TRAVELLERS NAME A CHEESE

## ❖ Stilton: King of English Cheeses

As if to prove that cheesemaking never stands still, two developments in Stilton, that most traditional of cheeses, have cheese aficionados excited. The first is that cheesemaking has returned to Quenby Hall, where many believe the first Stilton cheese was made. The second is that there is to be an unpasteurised Stilton again; although whether they will be allowed to call it Stilton remains to be seen.

Quenby Hall was magnificent as I drove up the long drive through an avenue of trees. Apart from the fact that the drive is now tarmac, the scene appears little changed from 1627, when the Jacobean hall was built by George Ashby in beautiful parkland some 10 miles east of Leicester. Freddie de Lisle, the present owner, set up a new dairy in 2005 where Sara Strong now makes Stilton again using milk from Tim Dixon's farm in the village.

Although cheese has almost certainly been made in the area since Norman times, the origins of Stilton, as we know it, lie sometime in the late 17th century, when the Ashbys at Quenby Hall were given a cheese recipe by one of their relations, Lady Mary Beaumont. The Ashby's housekeeper, Elizabeth Scarborough, made the cheese and it proved extremely popular when sold locally. When the Ashby family neglected Quenby in favour of their other estates, Elizabeth moved to Little Dalby. In 1720 she married a Mr Orton and started making cheese at Little Dalby Hall, where it is believed she perfected the recipe. The cheese was pressed and was consequently quite hard. It was probably blue more by accident than design.

At much the same time a Frances Pawlett was making a similar cheese in the nearby village of Wymondham. The story is hazy but it is thought that the Ortons and the Pawletts went into some sort of a partnership which included the owner of Quenby Hall and Cooper Thornhill, the landlord of The Blue Bell

Inn at Stilton. Quenby Hall, the Ortons and the Pawletts had the means to make the cheese and Thornhill had the perfect outlet to sell it.

The Blue Bell was a renowned inn on the Great North Road, the main London to York highway, where weary travellers – among them Dick Turpin, Lord Byron and Daniel Defoe - broke their journeys, changed horses and often stayed the night. As part of their meal they were usually served a fabulous cheese. Those who bought the cheese, thinking it had been made in Stilton, spread its reputation by that name. The first written mention of Stilton cheese is from Daniel Defoe who notes that in 1722 he "passed through Stilton, a town famous for its cheese". Its fame grew throughout the 18th century, as stagecoaches were used to transport vast quantities of the cheese for sale in London.

According to Ian Skailes, who is responsible for Cropwell Bishop, one of the best Stiltons produced today, the cheese these early travellers enjoyed bore little resemblance to today's cheeses. "They would have been much harder and drier" he says. Certainly this is borne out by Mrs Beaton, the great Victorian housewife, who referred to it as "British Parmesan" in her book of 1861, saying that it should be aged for 10 to 12 months or even longer. By contrast, today Ian Skailes' prize-winning Cropwell Bishop cheeses are aged for three months and are creamy and moist.

Stilton was the first English cheese to be awarded any sort of protection when, in 1910, the producers had the foresight to lay down some basic rules for its manufacture. These rules have served it well and it is unusual, today, to find any bad Stilton cheeses – not something one can say about Cheddar, that other pillar of English cheesemaking. True, the better cheeses come from the smaller dairies, like Cropwell Bishop and Colston Bassett, but even the big dairies produce cheeses which have some appeal. Dairy Crest, the largest Stilton producer, has experimented with automated production in their

Hartingdon dairy. The cheese vat is a moving rubber conveyor belt; the milk goes in at one end and cheese comes out at the other. Hardly romantic and, more to the point, relatively unable to respond to daily variations in milk supply; but the quality of the cheese remains consistently, at least, acceptable.

The rules for Stilton, now adopted into the European PDO system, state that it must be a "blue veined moulded cheese made in cylindrical form from full cream cows' milk with no added pressure and forming its own crust" from the geographical area of Leicestershire, Derbyshire and Nottinghamshire.

Most of the dairies I have visited, apart from the conveyor belt manufacture at Hartington, follow a similar pattern of make, which is roughly as follows. The milk, both morning and evening, is put in a large open vat and heated to about 30°c. The starter culture and penicillium mould spores are added. Rennet is added and the curd forms. After an hour or so it is cut and then left to rest for three hours after which the whey is drawn off and the curds transferred onto the cooling 'tables' which are really shallow vats. Depending on the maker this is sometimes achieved by letting the curds gently flow from the vat to the table by gravity. Sara at Quenby and Richard Rowlett at Colston Bassett prefer to ladle the curds by hand which they think is less rough on the curds. All are emphatic about the need for gentle handling.

Once on the table, the curds rest overnight when they are milled, salted and put into tall cylindrical moulds. The newborn cheeses go into the 'hastening room' where they are turned daily for five days, after which they are removed from their moulds and the sides of the cheeses smoothed with the flat blade of a knife. Some makers prefer to coat the cheese in cling film, which they believe achieves the same effect as smoothing with a knife but which I feel retains too much moisture in the cheese. After about six weeks, or roughly halfway through the maturing process, the cheeses are pierced with stainless steel needles. This process allows air to enter the centre of the cheese. The penicillium mould, which was added to the milk and has remained dormant, now turns blue with this exposure to the air and the maker is assured of a cheese with more evenly distributed blue veining than in days gone by, when the veining occurred largely by chance in any cracks and fissures which were in the cheese. A second piercing takes place a week or so later.

One area where the rules do not perhaps do the quality any favours is the insistence, since 1990, on pasteurisation. A cheese as traditional as Stilton, arguably Britain's King of Cheeses, should surely be made from raw milk. At present that is not so, but Randolph Hodgson and Joe Schneider intend to start making a blue cheese to a Stilton recipe from raw milk. Joe showed me round his new premises while the builders were busy laying the drainage in the floor. They have come to an arrangement with the owners of the magnificent 16,000 acre Welbeck Estate, built by the Dukes of Portland, in the north of Nottinghamshire and Joe is supervising the construction of his new dairy which they will call Stichelton. They will use the organic milk from the estate's herd of 150 Friesian cows.

Joe, who previously made Daylesford cheese, which is one of my very favourites for its stunning complexity and delicious flavours, is looking forward to the new challenge of making Stilton. He is an exceptionally skilled cheesemaker and is confident he can make a great Stilton. He adds with characteristic modesty that the recipe is, after all, very well known and that between himself and Randolph they are friendly with plenty of people who have a deep knowledge of the making and who are willing to help. His concern is more in the maturing and in ensuring the conditions are right for this to be achieved. From my previous knowledge of Joe I am sure he will succeed in making a truly stunning cheese and that it will be one of the most traditional cheeses made to a Stilton recipe. However there is a big question mark over whether he will be allowed to call it Stilton. I can't see why not — other than commercial interests of other makers — but signs are that the Stilton Makers Association will stop him, simply because he will make it from unpasteurised milk. Nevertheless I am really looking forward to tasting it. The renaissance of an unpasteurised organic Stilton is an exciting prospect.

Of the Stilton makers today, Colston Bassett and Cropwell Bishop are my two preferred cheeses. Each dairy takes its name from two villages which are close to each other in The Vale of Belvoir, some ten miles east of Nottingham. Colston Bassett is the smaller and more traditional of the two. Here Richard Rowlett, only the third manager in the history of the dairy, oversees a small workforce who follow much the same methods as were used when the dairy was founded in 1913, although they have pasteurised the milk since 1990. Recently I tasted the two cheeses together and both had their attractions. The Colston Bassett was very creamy, almost buttery, with a wonderfully full mellow flavour which lacked any harsh edges. The Cropwell Bishop, by contrast, also had plenty of flavour and was well balanced but, perhaps because it was a little younger, showed more of a mineral tang which was not unpleasant. Cropwell Bishop was quite ivory in colour and streaked with plenty of blue/green veining, whilst the Colston Bassett was white with more pin-point bluing. Both cheeses were quite moist and semi soft. In both the salt was quite subdued which is a pleasant change from some other blue cheeses. Neither was crumbly or acidic indicating that they were of sufficient maturity.

Driving round the countryside of Leicestershire, Nottinghamshire and Derbyshire one sees reminders of the rich heritage of coal and iron mining in the area. Surely these mineral deposits have their effect on the grazing, through the milk and into the cheese, manifesting themselves in the steely taste of a fine Stilton.

Some people only eat Stilton at Christmas time. This is a shame because it is excellent all year round. But, some of the best cheeses are made in September, when grass growth is good, and these mature just in time for Christmas.

The Victorians developed the custom of pouring port into Stilton. I don't recommend it. In my view it is a waste of two good products and the tradition probably originated when Stilton was a much harder cheese than today and the addition of port was a last desperate attempt to breathe some life into an otherwise dead and dry bit of cheese. Instead, if you a lucky enough to have a whole cheese, I advise you to cut off a disc about 1cm thick from the top, to form a lid, which can be used to keep the top surface covered. To serve the cheese remove the lid and cut wedges of 3-4 cm depth out of the top of the cheese. When you have cut wedges all round the cheese, start on the next layer. Cover the cheese with the lid after serving.

Today the village of Stilton seems an unprepossessing birthplace for what is, arguably, England's finest cheese. The wide High Street has a somewhat down-at-heel feel to it, with few shops or other signs of activity. However Liam McGivern, the present proprietor of The Bell Inn, keeps alive the spirit of its past with a warm welcome for travellers and locals alike.

## ❖ Other piquant blue cheeses

Bleu d'Auvergne is a reliable cheese from the Auvergne region of central France. Generally more moist than Stilton and slightly less creamy in taste, it has an appealing fresh acidity.

Also from the Auvergne, more mellow but otherwise quite similar is Fourme d'Ambert, which is produced in a distinctive tall cylinder shape.

A similar style cheese from Ireland is Cashel Blue. Named after the lovely town of Cashel where St Patrick made his speech about the three leaf clover being like the Holy Trinity, Cashel Blue was first made in 1984 by a husband and wife team, Jane and Louis Grubb, using the milk from their herd on a single farm in County Tipperary. The cheese has a certain sweetness to it and becomes increasingly soft and creamy with age.

Gorgonzola comes in two distinct styles, Piccante and Dolce. Piccante is considered the more serious cheese, and has a buttery texture with an appealing flavour neatly balanced between sweet and savoury. Dolce is much softer, almost runny, and is difficult to serve on a cheeseboard. It is an 'easy eating' cheese, great in sandwiches, as well as being useful as an ingredient in other dishes.

Cabrales is a cheese which evokes strong opinions because it is a powerful cheese with a persistent, intense flavour. It has a slightly granular, crumbly texture and is made in the Picos de Europa mountains of north-west Spain, traditionally from a mixture of cows', sheep and goats' milks.

Harbourne Blue is a relative rarity in that it is a blue cheese made from goats' milk. It has been made by Robin Congdon, in the supremely beautiful area of the Dart river estuary in south Devon, since the 1980's. It can be quite sharp and has a dry feeling texture in the mouth.

One of Robin's other cheeses is Beenleigh Blue which is, in effect, an English version of Roquefort, although it is less salty, perhaps more herbaceous and slightly sweeter.

Roquefort itself is impressive on a number of counts. Firstly for its sheer renown, throughout almost all the world; and every ounce, every kilo of Roquefort has passed through the small town of Roquefort in south-west France. To be precise, it has passed through and been matured in an area within the town some 300 metres by 2000 metres. It can be made throughout the Aveyron department, but it must mature for a minimum of 14 days in the natural caves of Combalou, Roquefort. Secondly, it is perhaps the original blue cheese. Certainly it has given its name to the strain of penicillium mould which creates the blue veining in nearly all blue cheeses - even Stilton. Allegedly some 2,000 years ago a local shepherd left his lunch of bread and cheese in a cave and returned some days later to find the cheese had turned blue, the action of natural moulds found in the cave. Thirdly, the site of the town itself is impressive. Perched precariously on the side of a steep rock face, it has grown up to give access to these natural caves which, with their specific geological structure, provide perfect conditions for maturing these cheeses to perfection. The cheese itself is only made from 1st December to 1st June each year. This is followed by a minimum of 14 days maturation in the caves at 6˚- 8˚c and then a further minimum of 3 months at a temperature of -3˚c, which may take place elsewhere in Aveyron. There are some 12 makers of which my three favourites are Carles, Vernieres Frères and Yves Combes. Roquefort has an ivory-coloured paste with many small holes coated in blue/green mould. Its flavour is herbaceous, sometimes slightly sweet and with an appealing tang. Too often it is over-salted. It is delicious with walnuts, perhaps in a salad.

## ❖ Taylor's 1977 Vintage Port

Stilton and a glass of Vintage Port is as fine a repast as one could wish for. It is a combination which has been enjoyed by generations ever since both were first made at around about the same time in the early part of the 18th century.

Of the two distinct styles of port, Vintage and Tawny, there is no doubt in my mind that Vintage is the better partner for Stilton. Tawny is simply too light for the task, but is ideally suited to other cheeses (see matching with Berkswell).

Described as 'The quintessential Englishman's wine', Vintage Port is only produced in years which are 'declared' by particular shippers when they consider the quality of the wines to be particularly good. Vintage Port is matured in vat for two years and then bottled while still young. Most of its maturing takes place in the bottle, which is slow – generally for at least 15 years. The resulting wine is full-bodied and robust, although with time the wines lose some of their initial power.

Vintage Port is the flagship by which many judge a port house and the success of the various houses varies from vintage to vintage. For me, and for many others, about the most consistent producer of top quality vintage ports is Taylor, Fladgate & Yeatman. Founded in 1692, for more than three centuries, the firm has been a leader in the port world. It is the last of the original English port houses to remain family owned. It has never been bought, sold or taken over. It is still run by descendents of the founders, with the present chairman being Alistair Robertson, who took over in the 1960's at the insistence of his aunt.

Alistair is proud of this heritage and keen to point out that family ownership has enabled Taylor's to be pioneers; they were amongst the first to buy wines in the Douro in the early 1700's, they were the first to buy a property there in 1744, they were the first to make a dry white port in 1934, the first to commercialise Single Quinta wines in 1958 and the first to introduce a Late Bottled Vintage Port with the 1965 vintage. They produce pretty well every style of port which is authorised but it is their Vintage Port which gives them such an outstanding reputation.

Taylor's Vintage Port is only made in years which they consider exceptional. The harvest usually takes place towards the end of September. At the Taylor's estates, pressing the grapes is still done by foot-treading in traditional stone lagares in order to extract the maximum colour and flavour from the grapes in the short fermentation time of three days, after which the addition of brandy stops the fermentation and retains some of the natural sweetness of the grapes. Soon after the harvest Alistair and his fellow partners including his son-in-law Adrian Bridge, Managing Director since 2000, and David Guimaraens, the partner responsible for winemaking, select the best wines from their two properties. These wines are then transferred to Taylor's maturing lodge in Vila Nova de Gaia, where they are left to age for two winters in large oak vats of some 15,000 litres.

In their second spring, they are tasted again and those vats which pass the test will be blended together to create Taylor's Vintage Port. Wines from Taylor's two vineyards go into the blend; David says that Quinta de Vargellas provides structure, elegance and complexity; Quinta de Terra Feita gives body, depth and powerful concentrated fruit.

When young, Vintage Port is one of the most inaccessible wines; sweet but austere, tannic, alcoholic, aggressive, massive in structure and very full-flavoured. It is quite an assault on both the mouth and the taste buds. David and his team have to assess these wines and decide which will develop into the great vintage ports on which Taylor's reputation hangs. Those selected will be bottled towards the end of their second year and laid down to await the judgement of wine merchants and writers, both those of today and those yet to come. Seldom is a vintage port ready for drinking in less than 10 years; usually it takes at least 15 to 20 years. Great vintages may not reach their peak for 30 or even 50 years and may still be enjoyed for years after that.

If Taylor's two vineyards produce wines of equal stature, there is no doubt that it is Vargellas, situated above a bend in the river, some 170 kms inland from Oporto in the wild and mountainous eastern extremity of the Douro valley, which is the spiritual heart of Taylor's. To be invited to Quinta de Vargellas is a treat; it is an enchanting mix of rural isolation and relaxed sophistication. Apart from vintage time, the area is almost deserted, utterly quiet, and if it were not for the neat rows of vines growing along man-made terraces hewn out of the rock, one would scarcely imagine man had ever been anywhere near the place. Walk from the dazzling sun of the vine-covered hillsides into the shade of Vargellas and immediately one is transported into quietly efficient comfort and elegance at odds with the rough, wild surroundings outside. A glass of chilled white or tawny port provides the perfect overture to a lunch or dinner. Fellow guests, drawn from a wide range of countries and backgrounds, appear and conversation flows along with the port; by the end of the meal one wonders why anyone ever leaves this idyllic place.

I drink Vintage Port for special occasions and so I don't mind the fact that it needs decanting an hour or so before drinking. In fact, the ritual is part of the enjoyment of the wine. Either I stand the bottle upright a day or so before drinking which allows the sediment to settle to the bottom, or I take the bottle straight from the rack and keep it virtually horizontal until I pull the cork. When I open the bottle depends on its age; an old wine need only be opened 30 minutes before drinking; a young wine may benefit from opening 2 or 3 hours before drinking. I have my decanter ready, with a funnel in its neck, to make pouring easier. I pull the cork as gently as possible so as not to disturb the sediment. I try to pour the port, again as gently as possible, with a steady hand, in one smooth single motion, very slowly. As soon as I see any sediment in the neck of the bottle or in the funnel, I stop pouring and the job is complete. Some people filter their port through a muslin cloth or even a coffee filter, but I feel this detracts from the quality of the port and should definitely be avoided.

Taylor's 1977 Vintage port marks my wedding year so I have always felt an affinity for it, but that apart, it is generally recognised as being a great vintage. Recently some wine critics have questioned its greatness and the price has fallen slightly. Others maintain that the best is yet to come from the wine and recommend keeping it until at least 2010. I regard this as good fortune because at the lower prices it is a cracking buy. In 2006 the wine was superb. It was beginning to turn slightly tawny at the edges but still retained a dark garnet colour at the centre. The nose was elusive but on the palate it was magnificent. Beautifully balanced, nutty but still with enough concentrated fruit. Velvety smooth, with no sign of excess alcohol.

When tasted with Cropwell Bishop and Colston Bassett Stilton, both cheeses tend to mask the port a little, but take another sip of the port and it comes right back in all its glory. I have no hesitation in recommending it.

At the same time I tasted the 1985 vintage. Clearly much younger, with evident berry fruit aromas, it was big and full bodied and initially stood up better to the Stiltons. But with each successive mouthful, my vote edged nearer to the 1977.

Of course, Taylor's 1977 is an expensive port, generally reserved for pretty special occasions; but there is no need to so restrict the eating of Stilton to special occasions. So what other ports could one enjoy with Stilton? My great favourite is a Single Quinta port. These are produced in exactly the same way as a vintage port but using grapes from just one quinta and in years which are not quite up to the quality demanded for a true vintage port. There are quite a few of these but just about the best is, not surprisingly, Quinta de Vargellas. Bought by Taylor's in 1893 when it produced 6 pipes of port, the vineyards now extend to 76 hectares and produce 204 pipes. The 1996 vintage is currently available at a fraction of the price of Taylor's 1985 or 1977. It is clearly still young with tannin still evident and would benefit from more ageing but, with its violety nose and complex concentrated fruity flavours with a hint of liquorice, it goes well with Stilton.

In my view, anyone seriously interested in good port should stick to the two styles I have covered in this book; Vintage (and here I include Single Quinta wines) and Tawnies aged to at least 10 years old. With these two styles of port you are in for many treats — without the hangovers. It is younger lower-quality ports which can cause a hangover. Avoid Late Bottled Vintage Port, which I regard as a bastardised invention to reduce the price of something which has a vintage on the label. Avoid also cheap Ruby ports and Tawny ports which do not have an age specification of at least 10 years. Colheita ports are unusual but can be good. They are Aged Tawny Ports from a single harvest.

For a special occasion the decanting and extra price of a good vintage port such as Taylor's 1977 are well worthwhile. For other occasions I get great pleasure from Quinta de Vargellas, which still needs decanting but is a fraction of the price, and from old tawnies, which do not need decanting and offer outstanding value for money.

If I have prevaricated over a definitive choice of Stilton and Port it is because all those I have tasted have something to recommend them. But for the very finest I would have little hesitation in choosing to eat a well-matured Colston Bassett Stilton whilst sipping a glass of Taylor's 1977 Vintage. To do so is to revel in two products which represent the very peak of their respective realms, which are both steeped in history and tradition and yet which, because quality is timeless, are as enjoyable today as ever they were.

# THANK YOU

I hope you have enjoyed reading this book; I have certainly had a lot of fun writing it. And I hope you have found some cheeses and wines which you would like to taste. Most are available in Britain, so do go out, buy some and try the combinations yourself. But don't stop there; there are plenty more cheeses and wines for you to experiment with, and you may find more stunning combinations; even some pairings which you prefer to the ones I have chosen. At the end of the day, it is all down to personal taste.

Thank you also to the cheesemakers and winemakers who welcomed me to their farms, dairies and vineyards; who told their stories and put me straight when I got the wrong end of the stick.

Many people have helped me in writing this book. I am extremely grateful to you all and I certainly could not have done it without you. First and foremost, my wife, Rachel, has given enormous support throughout, helping with tastings, photography and text reading; as well as sharing a life of cheese and wine.

My thanks go to Gerald Donaldson for offering the benefit of his vast literary experience and for introducing me to Philip Dodd who has been described as 'the Swiss Army knife of writing' because he can do everything.

Gloria Craven sweated over proof reading and pointed out my errors of grammar, spelling and simply where I failed to make sense.

Apart from the opportunities I have had, over the years, to taste some delicious food and wines, I have derived great pleasure from the people I have met along the way - colleagues, friends, customers, suppliers. Thank you all.

# GLOSSARY

| | |
|---|---|
| Affinage | The process of ripening or maturing cheeses |
| Alpage | The high mountain pastures where cows graze in summer |
| Annatto | A natural colouring dye derived from the plant Bixa Orellana |
| Au Lait Cru | French term for unpasteurised |
| B.Linens | A bacterium used to ripen washed rind cheeses, giving a golden colour |
| Brine | A solution of salt in water |
| Butt | The name given to casks in which sherry is stored. Each contains 490 ltrs |
| Curd | The coagulated solids from milk |
| Degorgement | The act of removing the sediment from a Champagne bottle |
| Dosage | The small dose of old sweetened wine which is added to Champagne just before bottling |
| Flor | Yeast which grows in the casks of some sherries and Chateau Chalon |
| Hastening Rooms | Stilton storage rooms where the curds bind together after cheesemaking |
| Lactose | Lactose is naturally present in milk and is converted into lactic acid by the starter culture |
| Lagares | A large shallow stone trough in which grapes are trodden by foot for the production of port wine |
| Lees | Sediment of yeast and solids from grapes |
| Milling | Chopping curd into small pieces or strips |
| Moule a la louche | French term for hand-ladled. The act of transferring the curds into moulds |
| Must | Grape juice |
| Penicillium | A family of moulds responsible for the blue veining in blue cheeses and the white fluffy rind on some soft cheeses. There are many strains |
| Pipe | The name given to casks in which port is stored. Each contains 550 ltrs |
| Quinta | Portuguese for farm |
| Remuage | The process of gently turning, shaking and inverting a bottle of champagne, so that the sediment lies on the cork |
| Rennet | A natural enzyme, found on the lining of calves' stomachs, which assists coagulation of the curds. Rennet substitutes are now sometimes used to make vegetarian cheeses |
| Starter Culture | A bacteria used to acidify the milk at the start of the cheesemaking process. Traditionally it would have occurred naturally at each farm. Now often freeze dried, although live, liquid 'pint starters' are preferred by many cheesemakers |
| Taille | The grape juice which comes from harder pressing of the grapes in Champagne. The first 80% is cuvee, the last 20% is taille |
| Tannin | A bitter chemical compound from grape skins, pips and stems and from oak casks, producing a drying, puckering effect in the mouth |

# INDEX